LETTERS TO THE PEOPLE OF INDIA
ON
RESPONSIBLE GOVERNMENT

LETTERS TO THE PEOPLE OF INDIA ON RESPONSIBLE GOVERNMENT

LIONEL CURTIS

GYAN

Published by

Gyan Publishing House
5, Ansari Road
Daryaganj, New Delhi-110002
Phone: 011-47034999, 9811692060
E-mail: books@gyanbooks.com

Distribution Network
gyanbooks.com
India, USA, Canada, UK, Australia

ISBN: 978-93-7133-597-3 (PB)

First Published, 1917

2nd Impression 2025

Printed at: Gyan Press, Delhi.

LETTERS TO THE PEOPLE OF INDIA ON RESPONSIBLE GOVERNMENT
Author Lionel Curtis

LETTERS TO THE PEOPLE OF INDIA ON RESPONSIBLE GOVERNMENT

By Lionel Curtis.

1917.

Preface.

As the Joint Address from Europeans and Indians to the Viceroy and Secretary of State has been coupled with my name in the Indian Press, I must briefly explain my connection therewith. Having made some studies of Indian Government more especially relating to the United Provinces, I submitted them for criticism to a number of Indians and Europeans for the purpose of verifying my facts and conclusions. Some of my friends who had read these studies, and were anxious that members of both races should agree in advising the Secretary of State, invited my assistance. I outlined a scheme, which I afterwards reduced to writing, but advised them to restrict their agreement to a few principles which seemed fundamental. They accepted this advice; but as it was desirable to promote discussion, the memorandum was published as well as the twelve points to which the signatories subscribed. It was made clear that the agreement related only to the twelve points and that the signatories remained free to differ on all the suggestions contained in the report by which it is prefaced. In the final draft of the twelve articles of agreement my advice was not taken on various points, though none the less I should have signed them as they stand, had I been qualified to do so by residence in India.

For the memorandum by which they are prefaced I accept the sole responsibility. For the sake of brevity it was condensed from materials accumulated in the course of a year's study of the subject, and a number of points raised in the discussions which took place, and in the documents submitted to the signatories, were omitted.

After its publication I was asked by some of the signatories, who rightly wished to promote reasoned discussion, to develop these points in a series of letters to the Press. Five such letters were published, and I must here acknowledge the kindness of Editors who printed them. It was not fair however to make such inordinate demands on their space as the subject required; and for studious readers the matter demanded presentment in more consecutive form. I therefore undertook to bring together what I had to say, including some matter already printed, in the form of a book. The work has had to be done at very short notice. The proofs have been read in haste, and those of the last few chapters I am not able to read at all. I must therefore ask my readers to excuse the blemishes which I expect to find when I see the book in published form. If these are not serious it will be due to the exceptional skill and care shewn by the printers in the hurried and difficult conditions under which their work has been done.

In order that the book may be published at the lowest possible price, some of the signatories have underwritten the cost. In the most unlikely event of any profit being realized, the amount will be paid over to war funds. I must none the less be held solely responsible for any opinions expressed in this book. The signatories are committed to nothing beyond the twelve articles they signed, and the *principle of specific devolution* upon which they are based. The virtue of that principle is its elasticity and the variety of ways in which it can be applied to all the varying conditions of India. As an illustration of this I append to the volume a suggestive scheme worked out by my friend Mr. Provash Chunder Mitter, which contains a wealth of information to which I cannot pretend.

The Congress-League Scheme and the Joint Address are also appended. The latter is printed from the types of the published edition, for greater facility of reference. Those to whom these documents are not already familiar should study them before attempting to read this book.

In conclusion, I must acknowledge the kindness of my friends Mr. Pugh, Mr. Arden Wood, and Mr. Harvey, in undertaking to pass this book through the press in my absence.

L. Curtis

December 17th, 1917.

Contents.

THE MEANING OF WORDS.

WHEN I first reached India in October 1916, there were two subjects of general discussion. One was the war; the other was self-government. Since the Proclamation which followed the Mutiny in 1858 the final aims of British policy in India had never been defined. The government of India for the good of Indians themselves was the principle which inspired that famous Proclamation. Its terms left for future interpretation the question wherein the good of Indians consisted. But since 1858 no further Proclamation had been made on the subject. Meanwhile the whole situation had been changed by the progress of education, and the British service found themselves forced by a situation in respect of which the supreme authority had left them without instructions. The British service were not to blame. It was the business of the British Parliament and electorate, and of no one else, to give them instructions, and none had been given.

Nevertheless self-government was discussed, in official as well as in Indian society, as the one conceivable goal of British policy. Everyone was talking of self-government last year; so I made it my business to discover what everyone meant by it, and I found no less than four different meanings, none of which conformed to my own conception of what the term, carried to its practical conclusion, must imply.

To begin with, there were British officials who talked of self-government. In answer to my questions I found that some of them meant no more than the emancipation of the Government of India from the control of Parliament and the Secretary of State, coupled with a devolution of specified powers and revenues to Provincial Governments. In the mouths of others it meant the re-partition of British India into Native

States. By self-government some Indians, as well as officials, meant no more than a progressive substitution of Indian for British officials. Fourthly, there were those who thought that executives in India could be left responsible, as at present, to the Secretary of State, and yet be rendered dependent for the exercise of their powers on Indian electorates and elected legislatures. This last alternative was the logical outcome of the Minto-Morley reforms.

The word self-government was used to include these four wholly distinct ideas, and the result, as it seemed to me, was that most people were talking at cross-purposes.

Some months later, I was obliged by circumstances over which I had no control to publish a letter dealing with the subject, and in speaking of self-government I felt bound to explain in unequivocal words the sense in which I used the term. With that object in view I recorded a conversation I had had with an able and responsible friend in one of the Native States. Let me quote the actual words which I wrote and published at that time.

> 'I suggested that a great deal of misunder-'standing was due to the fact that the term *self-gov-*'*ernment* was used to include two ideas (I have since 'found two more) which were in fact totally sepa-'rate. "In this State," I said, "you have gov-'"ernment of Indians by Indians. It is true you '"have some European officials who tell me that '"your Government is treating them well. But '"none the less the Government of His Highness '"the Maharaja is the government of Indians by an '"Indian. It is what we might appropriately call '"*Home rule*, if that name had not been assumed '"by a particular movement. But to shew you '"what I mean by self-government, let me ask you '"a question: Do you think that His Highness '"would be well advised to make the two follow-'"ing changes at once?—
>
> '"(1) To make the whole Legislative Council '"elective.

'"(2) To undertake to appoint as Diwan the "leader who commanded a majority of votes in "the Council, and also to dismiss him the mo-"ment he ceased to command a majority."'

'The most capable Indian administrators I have met are those who have gained their experience in the Native States, which proves the value of responsibility in training men. Some of them are men of the most liberal views, but I doubt whether any of them would think that so drastic a change can be made at one stroke. I think they would say that a Prince who made such a change too quickly would be likely to throw his State into confusion, and thereby delay its progress towards self-government. He would advise that several intermediate steps should be taken, and I think he would hesitate to name any exact time within which the final change could be brought about.

'Be that as it may, you will now see what I mean when I speak of self-government. To avoid the risk of this misunderstanding it will be better, I suggest, to drop this ambiguous term and to use the words *responsible government* instead.

'And now let me ask you to consider this system of responsible government as applied, not to a Native State, but to the vast and complicated structure of British India. Here you have two orders of government to deal with, the Government of India and also the various Governments of the Provinces into which India is divided. Personally I do not flinch from saying that I look forward to a time when in all these Provinces, and also in the capital of India itself, elective legislatures will sit, with executives wholly consisting of the leaders who for the time being command a majority, and resign the moment they cease to command it. . . .

'This is the end to which I am looking, and which can, I believe, be attained, if the goal is 'first clearly conceived, if the steps towards it 'are carefully thought out, if sufficient time is 'taken in making such steps, and also if each 'step is taken in time. I should find it difficult 'to suggest whether India has more to fear from 'over-haste or procrastination, and this I say, 'knowing that so wise, experienced and advanced 'a democrat as Lord Morley has spoken of that 'goal as one which may never be reached in India. 'With all due deference to an authority so 'weighty I believe that it can, must, and will be 'reached, and nothing which I have seen in 'India has shaken or is likely to shake that faith.'

II

THE PRONOUNCEMENT OF THE 20TH AUGUST.

In the last week of 1916 the Indian National Congress and the All-India Moslem League in their annual session at Lucknow resolved "that the time has "come when His Majesty the King-Emperor should be "pleased to issue a Proclamation announcing that it "is the aim and intention of British Policy to confer "Self-Government on India at an early date, ... and "that a definite step should be taken towards Self-"Government by granting the reforms contained in "the Scheme." This scheme the resolution then proceeded to give in detail. Some months later the Viceroy informed the Legislative Council that the Government of India had forwarded definite proposals for reform to the Secretary of State. Clearly some answer had to be given to the request tendered by the Congress and League before their next meeting. As a matter of mere courtesy they would have to be told whether their demand for a statement of policy was to be granted or not. Everyone, therefore, who had followed the course of affairs, had reason to know that some statement of policy was being considered, and might be expected at any moment. It was open to anyone to formulate and present their views as to what that statement should be.

On the 20th August the Congress and League received their answer. In form, as well as in substance, the answer differed from that suggested in their resolutions. They had asked for a Proclamation of the King-Emperor, such as that which was issued when Indian Policy had been last defined in 1858. The statement they got on the 20th of August was embodied in the form of an answer to a question in the House of Commons put to the Secretary of State for

India. The pronouncement was in substance the most important ever made on the place of India in the British Commonwealth. We cannot at this distance know what considerations induced a Cabinet, burdened with the exigencies of a terrible war, to make a pronouncement of such capital importance in a manner so unpretentious. Some allowance must be made for the difficulties which the Imperial Government has to face before we criticise the course they took. But to anyone, who knows anything of India, it must be a matter of regret that a pronouncement changing the whole direction of British Policy in India should have been made in a form so inadequate. Its significance must and will be determined by the gravity of the matter it contains. But that significance would have been far better understood by Europeans and Indians alike, had it been embodied in the form of a Proclamation, and, still more, had it been followed by such explanations by the Imperial Government and by the Government of India as its terms require. These terms are singularly plain. Yet dealing as they do with constitutional conditions new to India, their full significance has not been appreciated.

The pronouncement, of course, contains much that is not new. It reaffirms principles which have figured as common-places in the speeches of Secretaries of State and of Viceroys since the time of Lord Morley. Such for instance is the promise to increase the association of Indians in every branch of the Administration, and of the gradual development of self-governing institutions. The really new and therefore important matter was that contained in the words defining the goal to be sought. The Congress and League had asked the Imperial Government to proclaim "that it is the "aim and intention of British Policy to confer *Self-Government* on India at an early date." In the answer made to them on the 20th of August they got something else, and indeed more than they had asked for; and they got it in far more definite terms. The goal is stated as "the progressive realization of RESPON-

"SIBLE GOVERNMENT in India, as an integral part of the "British Empire." The words "Responsible Government" here appear for the first time in any official pronouncement on Indian Policy. I have seen it suggested in the Public Press that they were substituted by the Cabinet for the words "Self Government", used by the Congress and League, in a fit of absence of mind. As a glance at the first words of the pronouncement will shew, its terms were discussed in correspondence between the Imperial Government and the Government of India. The delay which took place, after the despatches of the Government of India were sent to London and before the Pronouncement was made, is sufficient evidence that every word was discussed and weighed. A writer who objects to "Responsible Government" as the goal of Indian Policy cannot get rid of it by imputing carelessness and levity to British statesmen. "Responsible Government" must have been used in the place of "Self-Government" with a full knowledge of the meaning it conveyed. Our first business, therefore, is to see what was the meaning which the Imperial Government must have attached to it.

All executives are of course responsible to some higher authority. The Governor-General in Council is responsible to Parliament in England. So were the executives of Ontario and Quebec in the time of Lord Durham, and those of the Transvaal and the Orange River Colony in the five years succeeding the War. They were so responsible because they could be dismissed and replaced by the Secretary of State acting as the Agent of Parliament. The demand arose in these countries (and at one time or another in all the self-governing Dominions), that the power of dismissing and replacing their executives should be taken from the Secretary of State and vested in their own electorates and in the Assemblies elected thereby. That demand has always been made in the name of Responsible Government. In the minds of men like Mr. Lloyd George and Lord Milner, in whose recollection the demands made and granted in South Africa are still fresh, the term cannot possibly have suggested anything else.

But the matter admits of no kind of doubt. Within the last few weeks the Lieutenant-Governor of the United Provinces, addressing the Convocation of the Allahabad University, used the following words:— "The British Government has announced that the "ideal for India is Responsible Government, which "means the administration of the country by an "executive authority responsible through an elected "legislature to the people; and we now have to shape "our course towards that goal."

An executive is only responsible to a higher authority when that authority can remove it and put another in its place. In this pronouncement the goal prescribed for India is identified with that already attained by the self-governing Dominions. It is to be reached as an integral part of the British Commonwealth. At present the Government of India and those of the Provinces are answerable to, and removable by, the British electorate through Parliament and the Secretary of State. The Imperial Government now looks forward to a time when those executives will all be answerable to, and removable by, Indian electorates, through elected Assemblies. It is added, however, that this goal can only be achieved "by successive stages." The British Government and the Government of India, in other words the Imperial Parliament and electorate, to which both these Governments are answerable, are to decide, from time to time, what those stages are to be and how fast they can be taken. But why are these stages needed? Why cannot the final power of removing and replacing these executives be transferred at one stroke from the Secretary of State to Indian electorates? The answer is contained in the words of the Pronouncement:— "The British Government and the Government of "India, on whom the responsibility lies for the welfare "and advancement of the Indian peoples, must be "judges of the time and measure of each advance, "and they must be guided by the co-operation received "from those upon whom new opportunities of service "will thus be conferred, and by the extent to which "it is found that confidence can be reposed in their "sense of responsibility."

In plain words, the British Government, at the moment of making the announcement, sees no electorates to whom it can transfer the responsibility which now rests on itself. The immediate task before it is to develop such electorates in India, and in such manner that it is possible to test the reality of the development. The question how this is to be done is the root of the whole problem set by the Pronouncement of the Imperial Government.

Short of a pronouncement involving the separation of India from England, no declaration of policy more definite and final could have been made. From public statements we know that its terms were under discussion between the Imperial Government and the Government of India since the earlier months of this year. We know that Mr. Montagu engaged to take up matters where Mr. Chamberlain left them; nor is it unlikely that when the records are laid bare, the future historian may find the pronouncement, as issued on the 20th of August, amongst the papers of Mr. Chamberlain. In any case it was accepted by a Cabinet which includes not only a Liberal Prime Minister and a Labour member, but Lord Curzon, Lord Milner and Sir Edward Carson. It was tacitly accepted by the House of Commons and by the House of Lords. Its announcement to Parliament without provoking a vote of censure is equivalent to its acceptance by the Imperial Parliament and electorate. It is now, despite the casual form in which it was announced, in every way a pronouncement of the Imperial Government, a British declaration of policy. It was made by the lawful and accredited Government of a people now in arms to vindicate the word they plighted to the Belgian Nation. If I know our people, they will not go back on their word. It reflects moreover their innermost mind. In the last few days I have listened to one, unconnected with party or press, who was recently sent to discuss public affairs with the men in the trenches on the Western front. To his questions about India he was met with the answer, "Well, we know little about India. But we're fighting for the British Empire, which stands for self-government, and it's up to England to help India to self-government. That is the principle for which we are fighting."

In the last few weeks I have read and listened to suggestions that this declaration of policy was wrung from England by fear. Would Indians, who have said such things in Calcutta, repeat them within the sound of the guns, to those who stand in the presence of death, to whom the word 'fear' cannot be named? By such words they dishonour not England, but themselves. Not once nor twice in this country have I felt how little they know of India, who only India know. Englishmen must learn to know India better, but to know India you must also know what England is, and that knowledge must be sought in the shambles of Flanders and France.

For the moment, however, I am speaking to my own countrymen in India. Whether it will ever be possible to transfer the control of all Indian affairs to Indian Electorates, and to place India on the same footing as the self-governing Dominions, is a point upon which some of us may differ. But on one point we shall all agree, that unless or until that goal can be reached, the final decision of British Policy in India must rest with the Imperial Government, Parliament and electorate, which for the present is the British Government, Parliament and electorate. Such decisions cannot rest either with Indians, nor yet with the British community in India. But what both communities can do is to give public opinion in England the information it sadly needs, and give it in time. So far the information available there has been drawn from two sources, and two only: from Nationalist quarters and from British officials. From missionary circles little has been heard, and from business circles in India, till the last few months, nothing at all. I am not questioning the truth of what Nationalists say, or what the officials say. But I do say that the picture placed before the people of England is utterly incomplete, unless it includes information other than that derived from Nationalist and official quarters.

It is for this reason, I believe, that everyone in England will welcome the sudden awakening of their unofficial countrymen here to an interest in public affairs. For the moment the trouble is that that awakening has come too late. A new declaration of policy had been long pending and promised: but the views of the European community were not expressed, until it had been made in terms which are now impossible to alter.

In future the people of England will, one hopes and believes, receive the advice of their countrymen here. The effect of that advice will surely depend on its quality and motive. If it is solely concerned with the interests and privileges of Englishmen in India it will, I predict, weigh but lightly. If on the other hand it comes from men, who are keeping in view the interests of India and of the whole British Commonwealth, and who speak with knowledge, not only of their own business concerns, but also of the public trust which England is seeking to discharge in this country, such advice will, I believe, weigh with preponderant force. The time has come when your countrymen at home are entitled to have your opinions on subjects like commercial representation, and the separation of executive and judicial functions. India is not Morocco, nor the Argentine, nor Korea, but an integral part of the British Commonwealth, and the time is past when Englishmen here could confine themselves to business, as though public questions in India could be settled on none but official advice. And therefore the time is past when the European Association could stand only for securing the privilege of Europeans in India.

With all this I know you will agree. But there is another and even graver point. From time to time England must make decisions, and give pledges with regard to her policy in India,—such pledges as were given in 1858, and once again on the 20th of August last. You at least know the value of British prestige, which rests simply on India's faith in the two Saxon words 'Yea' and 'Nay.' In the end England will be judged in India by what England herself does, or leaves undone. But at any given moment the people of England largely stand to be judged by their fellow countrymen who are face to face with Indians themselves. The men who return from the trenches will, I believe, see that this promise is kept. Let their countrymen here think twice before assuming positions which must lead Indians to think that Englishmen at home may be made to play fast and loose with their pledges. Those pledges are given to you no less than to Indians, and they also will be making a vast mistake, if they dream that after the war England can be brought to change or go back on one phrase or word of this solemn Pronouncement.

That is the main point. But now there is a kindred point, which I commend to the notice of Indians as well as to my own countrymen at this juncture. The Pronouncement is binding on the Secretary of State *in all its terms*. Under them he was sent here by the Imperial Cabinet, and, as I read them, it is not permissible for him to discuss whether such a declaration should have been made, whether responsible government is a feasible project in India, or whether, let me add, it can be granted outright, or otherwise than by a succession of steps. His enquiry is limited to the four corners of that Pronouncement. The advice he must seek is simply how effect may be best given to it. If this interpretation is right, it follows that everyone who feels he has views to offer at this juncture, should consider whether the Pronouncement is one which he can accept, and whether the views he has to offer are within its terms. It is perfectly open to any one, British or Indian, to say that he does not accept its terms: such views can be addressed to the Imperial Government, to Parliament and the public in England with whom the ultimate decision lies. But the Pronouncement shews that the

Secretary of State has not been empowered to discuss such views. Surely he is limited by its terms to proposals which can be brought within the lines laid down for him by the Imperial Government before he left England. And the limitation is two-edged. Advice to do nothing, and proposals to grant responsible government outright, are in fact demands that the Pronouncement should be changed, and that new instructions should be issued to the Secretary of State. I venture to predict that it will not be changed, and that these instructions will bind not Mr. Montagu only but all Secretaries of State in time to come until, by successive stages, Responsible Government had been realised in India.

III

ELECTORAL SYSTEMS FALSE AND TRUE.

The steps by which the goal is to be reached, and especially the first of those steps to be taken, which must of necessity determine the character of all those which are to follow, are left for subsequent inquiry. The question before us is simply that of discovering the path whereby that goal can be reached most quickly. But in order to do that we must begin by glancing at the point from which we are to start. Except in the district and municipal boards, there are no executives removable at the will of electorates. So far as the Indian and Provincial Governments are concerned, responsible government has no place in the existing constitution. In the last few years an Indian member has been appointed to each of the executive councils, but his responsibility to the Secretary of State differs in no respect from that shared by his European colleagues. Like them he is called to office, and can be dismissed, by the Secretary of State.

The legislatures consist partly of officials, who in the Governor-General's Council only are in the majority, partly of non-officials, mostly Indians, appointed by Government, and partly of members, almost entirely Indian, who do not hold their seats by government appointment. From the latest returns it appears that the Imperial Council consists of 68 members, 27 of whom are elected. Of these 18 are elected to speak for sectional interests, either land-holders, Mahomedans, merchants or manufacturers. The remaining 9, indirectly elected by non-official members of the nine Provincial Councils, are presumably intended to voice the views of the people at large.

To illustrate the method of election, let us take the case of the member representing the United Provinces. His constituency consists of the 29 non-official members of the Legislative Council of that Province. Of these 29 members, 21 are elected. Of the 21 elected members, 8 represent sectional interests, and 13 the District and Municipal Boards. Of the 13, only 4 are directly elected by the Boards. The remaining 9 are returned by electoral colleges composed of delegates elected by District and Municipal Boards in each of nine Divisions. The Boards are directly elected; so at last we come to the bed-rock of primary voters. The voters to the District Board are simply nominated by the Collector. But he may not nominate more than 100 for any one tahsil, which means in practice not more than one in every 2,000 inhabitants. Educated Indians are accused of seeking an oligarchy under the guise of Self-government. Here, in a law made by ourselves, the image of oligarchy was stamped on the system. This iron limitation is enough to shew how little the fundamental problem of developing electorates figured in the minds of those who elaborated this travesty of an electoral system.

We are now in a position to trace the electoral chain by which a member of the Imperial Council is supposed to represent a voter in one of these Divisions.

1. The primary voter returns a member to the District or Municipal Board.
2. The Boards return members to an Electoral College.
3. The College returns a member to the Provincial Council.
4. The non-official members, including sectional members and those appointed by Government, return a member to the Imperial Legislative Council.

The system is one which destroys any real connection between the primary voter and the member who sits on the Legislative Councils. Repeatedly have I asked those in a position to know, whether a primary voter casts his vote with any reference to the effect it will have in determining the composition of the Legistive Councils. The answer was always in the negative.

For all practical purposes, the non-official members of the Provincial Councils are primary electors, so far as their representatives in the Imperial Council are concerned. They hold no mandate from those who elect them. Their position as elected members is purely and simply a voter's qualification, which takes the place of age, property, education, or any of the ordinary qualifications of voters. One member in the Imperial Council sits by virtue of a majority of 9 votes. The total number of votes, by which all the elected members of this Council are returned, can scarcely exceed 4,000. That gives less than an average of 150 for each member. Similarly, members of the Legislative Council of the U.P. are elected by about 3,000 votes, or an average of about 143 for each elected member.

From this analysis, it is plain that, so far as the Legislative Councils are concerned, the so-called representative system is a sham. The experience it provides can do little or nothing towards developing electorates, for the reason that the primary voter for the District and Municipal Boards cannot possibly trace the effect of his vote on the Legislative Councils. Lord Morley failed to see that this was the crux of the problem, because he would never face in his own mind the prospect of devolving responsibility on Indian electorates, as the Imperial Government has now faced it. Hence the practical importance of the recent pronouncement.

Let us now turn to this essential question, the development of electorates, and see what answers have been given to it. One answer commonly given is that no political responsibility can be given to electorates, until education is far more advanced and more widely spread than it now is. Implicit in this answer is the presumption that the future electors can be educated to a sense of political responsibility in schools and colleges. My answer is that if you were to cover India with schools and colleges until you had multiplied the educated classes tenfold, without at the same time giving them any instalment of genuine political responsibility, you would have rendered India ungovernable under any system. This I believe is exactly what has happened in Russia. There, public responsibility was limited to Municipal and District Bodies. In the Imperial and Provincial Governments, the educated classes were confined to criticising the executives, over whom they had no control. In the political sphere they were left without responsibility for seeing that the government was carried on. The natural result is that they have been able to destroy government, but have proved utterly incapable of evolving any government of their own, which they could bring themselves, let alone the illiterate majority, to obey. The results are before us, if only in the awful silence which envelops Russia, and recalls those hours in the Black Hole of Calcutta. So deadly and so general is the struggle of each for himself, that no one is able to tell those without of the tragedy in progress within. May the wisdom of her rulers deliver India from a like fate! But that cannot be done by denying education to her people. They must have education, and more and more of it, but the result will be the same as in Russia, unless side by side with increasing education is given a steady and progressive increase in political responsibility.

The truth is that schools and colleges can do no more than teach people how to learn They can impart knowledge, but wisdom can only be learned in the school of responsibility. It can only be taught by leaving men to suffer by the results of the things which they themselves do; still more, by the results of the things which they leave undone.

Last year I visited a village in Central India where some people had died of cholera. The villagers had promptly gone to the police station, obtained permanganate of potash, put it in the wells and stopped the cholera. The Commissioner, with whom I was camping, told me that only a few years before the police had been mobbed for attempting to disinfect the wells. The change had come about, because, in their own experience, they had seen that permanganate in the wells will stop cholera. Now let anyone consider whether this practical truth would have come home to them, if it had only been taught them in text-books. School teaching will help to disintegrate the deadening effect of custom, to open the eyes of the mind to new ideas, and enable a community to read the lessons of experience more quickly. But the practical lessons of life must come from experience itself. Without experiencing the results that follow the giving of votes, under a system so simple as to make that experience easy to read, education will operate to unfit a people for responsibility in public affairs. The two things must go side by side. The educational value of the present electoral system is destroyed by its complication, and also by the fact that members have no function but criticism, and no responsibility laid upon them. And hence there is none laid upon the voters. But their judgment cannot be developed except by a system which enables them to trace the results of their votes on their own lives; in plain words, by some responsibility.

In the making of electorates, a quality more difficult to develop, even than judgment, is discipline. The hardest lesson a raw electorate has to learn is that of giving the rulers they elect power to rule. The obedience upon which government is founded, even in Autocracies, is at root moral. Despotism rests on a basis of theocracy, on the idea of a law delivered on Horeb. The obedience rendered by his subjects to an Indian Prince is inspired by the belief in his divine title to rule. It is not force which makes the Indian peasant so docile to British rule, so much as an ingrained conviction that power to rule is of itself an evidence of divine authority. To this title the Kaiser is constantly appealing. It has enabled the Czars to rule Russia for centuries. But the idea is one which will not stand the disintegrating force of education. If relied upon too long, it suddenly collapses, as in Russia. And then a people undisciplined by any sense of responsibility, outside the sphere of district, village or town life, are called upon to obey men elected to rule the Province and the Nation. The old principle of obedience is suddenly shattered, before they have had time to acquire the only alternative principle, which is the habit of obeying rulers in the general interest and because they represent the general authority. Self-government rests on a sufficient capacity in enough individuals to put the interests of others before their own. It is the Sermon on the Mount reduced to practice in the field of politics. This habit can, I firmly believe, be produced in any people by constant and increasing exercise. But it is contrary to all reason and all experience of human nature to suppose that it can be produced without the exercise of responsibility, steadily increased as the habit becomes more fully acquired and more widely spread. Mr. Montagu's mission is the necessary corollary of that undertaken by Dr. Sadler and his colleagues.

To put the matter in a nut-shell, the view—long current—that an improvement and extension of education is the key to the political problems of India, is a dangerous half-truth. It is but a fragment of the true key, and if tried alone, will break, with the results inevitable when a lock is jammed by a broken key.

IV

THE EXISTING SYSTEM AND ITS LOGICAL OUTCOME.

The best that can be said of the existing system is that it has introduced to the legislatures an element whose point of view is other than that formed in official experience. I believe that legislation and public policy have benefited by the public criticism of laymen. But it trains those laymen merely as critics. It provides no training in, and no test of, administrative capacity or statesmanship. The leaders who emerge and figure in the public eye are necessarily those who can criticise most effectively in the English tongue. They are never put to the test, nor trained by the necessity of having to do anything themselves.

In all Provincial Councils non-officials are in the majority. In Bengal the elected members alone are in the majority.

To these majorities are opposed a minority of British officials bound by the express orders of the Government of India to vote, in every division, in accordance with orders issued by Government. I do not know the reason for these orders. In the Transvaal and Orange River Colonies, where I watched the same system under Crown Colony government, officials were left free to vote according to their own judgment on all but questions of primary importance, those, generally speaking, which, under responsible government, might involve a change of the ministry. I do not think the Government whip was issued on half a dozen divisions in the session. Official members were free to speak, and in doing so often influenced the Government in the direction desired by the non-official members. In the Indian Councils no official may speak, except at the instance of the Executive. In the Transvaal there was no such cleavage as exists in India between official and non-official members.

The whole effect of this system strikes one as singularly calculated to produce a cleavage on racial lines, and to exasperate racial feeling. Inevitably it operates to produce a solidarity of Indian members, on purely racial lines, in opposition to an alien Government, and the cases in which Governments are defeated are steadily increasing. In plain words, moderates are forced into the camp of extremists.

If Government proposes unpopular measures, or resists popular resolutions and amendments, it is not because it likes doing unpopular things. Unrepresentative governments are far more nervous of opposition than those which rest on an ascertained majority of voters. Government only resists the elected members where it is honestly convinced that it cannot otherwise discharge the trust laid on it, and in the last instance because it cannot otherwise maintain order. Already Provincial Governments are directly dependent on non-official votes for the concurrence of the legislature, without which they cannot discharge the duties laid on them. Is it humanly possible, if this system be long continued, that the Executives will resist the temptation to influence non-official members by means other than pure argument in open debate? Wherever this system has been long continued, government by "influence" has set in, degenerating into government by intrigue, and ending in government by corruption.

How far Executives are still able to maintain a working majority it is difficult to say, because they shrink from proposing necessary measures which mean public defeat. But where they do succeed in voting down the elected members, the spectacle of the British phalanx casting a solid vote against them by order is irritating in the extreme. Inevitably it begets a demand for a clear and overwhelming elective majority, as the natural means of relief from the exasperation felt on being voted down by British officials. The present system suggests to Nationalists a line of advance which will enable them to tie the hands of the Executive without assuming any responsibility for the results of inaction.

The schemes suggested by Mr. Gokhale, the nineteen members, and by the Congress and League, are the logical result of this situation. With one exception, to which I propose to refer later on, all the schemes for development on the lines initiated in the Morley-Minto reform proceed on this principle of strangling the responsible Executive by successive twists of the noose placed in the hands of irresponsible electorates. I have before me a letter from one of the ablest administrators in this country in which he rejects any scheme for the gradual delegation of specified functions on Provincial authorities responsible to electorates. He goes on to say: "I feel that it should "not be beyond the wit of constitutional experts to "frame a scheme of advance along the road of hori-"zontal lines of increasing popular control over all the "functions of government instead of vertical lines sepa-"rating particular functions and without reaching a "chasm that must be crossed at one bound."

I propose therefore to examine this idea of increasing popular control on horizontal lines in the case of the existing executives and legislatures. Let us take the Executive first. The vital question, I submit, by which any scheme of government should be tested is this—*to whom is the Executive under that scheme to be made responsible for their final decisions?* There are two alternatives and two only: Executives may remain responsible to the Secretary of State, which means to the Imperial Parliament, or else they may be made responsible to an electorate in India. There must and should be divisions in electorates and legislatures. In Executives there can be none, so far as the public is concerned. All experience demonstrates that, unless government is to come to a standstill, the members of executives must thrash out their differences within closed doors. When a member of an Executive Council is voted down, he has but two courses before him: to resign, or else to support the decision of his colleagues, if only by his silence loyally observed in private as well as in public. Mr. Balfour once declared that he had often supported in public debate proposals which he had opposed in the privacy of the Cabinet. Every man with experience of public affairs knows that this is an essential condition of executive action. Before a member of an Executive is at liberty to explain his differences with his colleagues he must quit it. They must cease to be colleagues. In Executives there must be unity, and it is for that reason that the selection of his colleagues is usually left to the head of the government. The principle of electing the Cabinet by the caucus of the party in power, introduced in Australia, has now, I believe, been discarded as incompatible with the unity of the Cabinet.

Proposals are on foot to introduce two Indian members into the Executives here, and I very much hope they will be adopted. But the suggestion that these two members should be elected by the non-official members strikes at the root of the first principle of executive government Responsibility of an Executive means that the members of that Executive are appointed and can be removed by the authority which appoints them It means therefore that they must be able to explain their conduct to that authority. This proposal means that while three members of an Executive Council are to remain responsible to the Secretary of State, the two others are to be made responsible to the elected members. When they differ from their colleagues they are placed in a wholly false position. If they are loyal to their colleagues, they cannot explain their position to their electorate. Nor can they explain their position to their electorate without divulging the secrets of Council. And if, to escape the falsity of this position, they resign, how then are their places to be filled? The same electorate can only return two new members charged to maintain the difference with those responsible to the Secretary of State. Such an arrangement can be fruitful in nothing but misunderstanding and anger, leading to deadlock. If, as I hope, there are to be more Indian members, they must be appointed by the Secretary of State, and be responsible to him on the same footing as their colleagues. Or else they must all be responsible to an electorate on the same footing.

We may now turn to plans for increasing control over all the functions of government as applied to the existing legislatures. The steps which can be taken in this direction are few and easy to trace.

The first step is to give the elected members a clear and decisive majority.

The second step is to divide the estimates into two sections, one containing police and other items of vital importance, to be reserved as at present to the control of the Executive; the other section containing items which are left at the disposal of a legislature in which elected members have the decisive voice.

The third and last stage is to submit the whole budget, that is to say supply, to the control of the legislature.

To begin with, it is necessary to note that the word "control" may mean either of two things. It may mean the power of deciding that things are to be done. It may also be used to mean a power of deciding that they are not to be done. If the fabric of society is to be maintained, the Government must in the last resort have power to do anything necessary to maintain it. Before taking a decision, it may expose itself studiously to the influence of external opinion. It may modify its policy in a great variety of details to meet a great variety of views. But in the last analysis it will be faced by the necessity of making decisions which conflict with certain feelings and views. There may be all kinds of knowledge which a Government lacks and which outside opinion can supply. But there is a kind of knowledge which actual responsibility, and that alone, can supply. A Government which cannot or will not in the last resort apply that knowledge, and interpret it into action, is doomed; and the community it governs is also doomed to anarchy. A Government may know that order cannot be enforced, unless criminals are convicted, and that criminals cannot be convicted, unless adequate protection can be given to witnesses. The existing law may not enable them to give this protection. The law must be changed, and, unless the necessary legislation can be passed, crime will increase until social order is destroyed. In England a Government, which cannot pass such legislation as it feels to be necessary, resigns. Another assumes its responsibility; and that responsibility brings the same knowledge, until both parties are convinced by experience of the necessity of making the change in the law required. But in India the existing executives cannot be removed by the legislatures, and, if they are to maintain order, cannot be divested of power to pass necessary laws however unpopular. They may and should be exposed to the influence of public opinion to the utmost. But in the last analysis they must have the power to decide which responsibility for maintaining order places upon them. The control which a Government must have cannot be divided. It can only be undermined and gradually destroyed.

The first step in all these schemes is to give the elected members a clear and decisive majority. When this is done there is no reason for keeping a small phalanx of official voters, who are not needed to speak, at the disposal of Government. They are not needed when measures are popular; they are perfectly useless when measures are resented. Indeed, they are worse than useless, because their presence is exasperating. Mr. Gokhale proposed that the official members should not be more than were necessary for explaining the Government case. He seems to have realized that their votes cease to have any value as a safeguard the moment they are reduced to a clear minority. The proposal to give a clear, decisive majority of elected members is equivalent to placing the Executive at the mercy of a wholly elective Council, unable to change the Government and with no responsibility for seeing that it is carried on. The question which ought to be considered is whether any Government under any circumstances ought to face that position.

I know what is in the back of the minds of some of those who advocate such measures. They believe that the "influence" of Government with a balance of members will suffice to secure them enough votes on most critical divisions. In its power of patronage, and of conferring titles and dignities, any Government in India has means of influence far greater than exist elsewhere. It is the most upright Government in the world; and yet, if you put it in such a position, it will infallibly yield to such temptation, without realizing, to begin with, that it is doing so. In any case it will suffer from the belief in the minds of its opponents that such means are used. In India, it cannot escape that imputation. Under the existing system, the imputation is already being made.

The above remarks apply to the first stage, that in which the control of legislation is abandoned by the Executive to the elected majority of the legislature. We now come to the second stage, that in which the Executive retains control of funds needed for police and other vital services, while abandoning the appropriation of the balance of the revenue to the elected members. To begin with, this concession is largely illusory, because the real bone of contention is the allocation of funds between police and education, that is to say, between the two different sections of the estimates. The arrangement will not prevent elected members from attacking the Executive for appropriating too much revenue for police, and for leaving too little for the heads submitted to the control of the legislature. The President can scarcely rule such speeches out of order. They will figure conspicuously in every budget debate, and help to aggravate the public temper. Now it is noticeable that, in the Provincial legislatures, attacks on the Government of India for their military expenditure play little part, and unless sufficiently veiled, could be ruled out of order from the chair. In the District Boards attacks on the Provincial Government for not reducing police expenditure, in order to give the Boards more revenue for education, are not heard at all.

One reason is that the financial relations of the province with India, and those of the district with the province, are settled by contracts covering a period of years. But the division of the revenue into two parts, one reserved to the control of Government, and the other submitted to the control of the legislature, can scarcely be made on a fixed basis. It will have to be adjusted every year, and the readjustment will be the occasion of most exasperating discussions.

The Executive know that if they are to do their duty and to maintain order, they must spend so much on police. They cannot afford the balances demanded by the elected members for their own section of the estimates, without imposing new taxation. If elected members wish to spend more money on education, there must be fresh taxation. Now it is a sacred principle of public finance, in the most democratic countries of the British Commonwealth like Australia, that proposals for new taxation must be initiated and framed by the ministers of the Crown, and not by private members in the legislature. The Executive may listen to suggestions from the legislature, but the formal proposal must be made and embodied in a Bill by the Executive. In India, at any rate, the whole responsibility for the new tax, and all the unpopularity accruing therefrom, will rest on the Executive.

The able administrator, whose proposals I am criticising, remarks: "No official can satisfactorily "serve two masters whose instructions will be conflict-"ing, without neglecting the interests of one." It will readily be seen, however, that the proposal to divide the estimates into two parts violates this principle. The Executive is to reserve control over one part of the estimates, yielding control of the other part to the legislature. The Executive is to be responsible to the Secretary of State for one part of the estimates, and to the legislature for another part. For the legislators have no other Executive of their own. To give them a separate Executive for the matters assigned to their control is the very proposal which my critic condemns.

So much for the second stage; and now we come to the third and last stage, that in which the legislators are given the whole control of supply as well as of legislation, the Executive still remaining responsible to the Secretary of State. The Executive can pass no laws, and obtain no money, except by the will of an elected legislature. But the legislature cannot remove the Executive. The Government is only removable by, and is, therefore, still responsible to, the Secretary of State. Of such an arrangement it can only be said that it must from its nature lead, and has in experience always led, to a constitutional deadlock, the paralysis of government and consequent social disorder. The results of such a condition in a country like India can best be judged by those who have spent their lives there.

So far I have been discussing proposals, which are the necessary and logical outcome of the Minto-Morley reforms. Schemes devised on that principle differ mainly in the distance they propose to go down one and the same road which ends in a precipice. The Congress-League scheme would lead India to the very brink. To take one of its provisions only, it is laid down that Executives, whether National or Provincial, are bound by a resolution twice passed within thirteeen months, despite the veto of the Governor-General. Let us take two not improbable cases. Suppose that a resolution is twice passed, obliging the Executive to make primary education universal and compulsory within a given time Such a step would involve a vast increase of taxation. But the whole onus of framing the necessary measures of taxation is left to the Executive. That the legislature would shrink from passing such measures is more than probable. The Executive would then be in a position of having to execute orders, without the means of doing so. The legislature is to have power of issuing orders without the obligation of providing the funds to pay the cost. Such a scheme is impossible from the outset. It is also the negation of responsible government.

Then again the legislature might order the Executive to reduce the expenditure on police by one half. Such orders might involve an actual violation of contracts legally binding on Government. It might also, in the judgment of the Executive, involve an outbreak of public disorder. The opinion of the Governor-General would already have been recorded in his abortive veto, which would certainly not have been given without reference to the Secretary of State. As public-spirited and honorable men, the Executive, and indeed the Governor-General himself, would have no choice but to resign. The Secretary of State could not find others to take their place, and, without violating his conscience, could not ask them to do so. A deadlock with all its perils would be the result. "I would press," writes one of the advocates of this scheme, "for substantial control of Government until we can "get responsible government. The step from the "former to the latter will not be a long one." *

As one who desires to see responsible government established in India as quickly as possible, I venture to differ. Responsible government can and will be attained by straightforward means. It will not be attained by means designed to destroy all government in the process.

The vital defect of the Minto-Morley principle is that it leaves the whole responsibility for government on one set of men, while rapidly transferring power to another set of men. It operates to render electorates less fit for responsible government, instead of more so. It creates a situation eminently calculated to exasperate the Executive and legislature with each other, and therefore to throw the British Government and the Indian community at large into a posture of mutual antagonism. The elected members, untempered by any prospect of having to conduct the government themselves, have everything to gain by harassing Government, and preventing it from passing the measures which it knows to be vital. In actual practice what happens, is not that Government is defeated,

* Letter to the *Bengalee* dated November 22, 1917.

but rather that it shrinks from proposing measures which it knows it cannot pass. The nerves of the State are slowly but surely paralysed. The elements of disorder grow and raise their heads. Every necessary measure for preserving order is denounced as an act of tyranny. The foundations of law decay, until suddenly, as in Ireland, the whole structure collapses, order has to be restored at the cost of bloodshed, and the growth of constitutional government is indefinitely postponed. No Government suffering from creeping paralysis can maintain its prestige. Even in India the prestige of Government does not depend upon outward show, upon ceremonies, uniforms, salutes, and the like, but simply on ability to discharge its functions. I regard the future establishment of responsible government in India as the greatest achievement in which my own race can share. But Government, as the leaders of the Russian revolution are discovering, is the only possible basis of self-government. Home rule can be given to Scotland or Wales, if they asked for it, to-morrow. The real difficulty of giving it to Ireland is that Government has never been firmly established in that country. In India no measures are real steps to self-government which operate to render it ungovernable in the process. Under the plan proposed, no elective member of the legislature contracts any responsibility for the maintenance of order. He merely develops into a hostile critic of the Government's endeavour to do so. He is given no chance of demonstrating any capacity to get things done. Popular leaders are brought to the front mainly by ability to harass the Government in trying to do them. There is no gradual transfer of responsibility. When public irritation has been raised to boiling point, and the final deadlock is reached, the only further concession which remains is to make the Executive responsible to, and therefore, removable by, the legislature. This means the institution of responsible government at one stroke in a community where electors and legislators have been given no previous exercise in political control. The intermediate stage of divided control is so eminently calculated to produce public irritation that it would, in my opinion, be far safer to take this step at the outset. That course, however, is specially rejected in the recent pronouncement of the Secretary of State; so it does not therefore come within the scope of these notes to discuss it.

V

THE FRUITS OF EXPERIENCE.

The fact is that no system will succeed under which it is not possible in the last instance to secure harmony between the Executive and legislature in matters essential to government. The discovery of the means whereby this can be done in a Government based on election is the great achievement of England; and it is worth while glancing at the manner in which that discovery was arrived at. In the early Middle Ages, the King ruled and enacted the laws. Then came the stage at which Parliament had acquired the sole right of making laws and voting supply, while the executive power remained in the hands of the King and his ministers. There were no legitimate means of harmonising the action of the Executive and legislature, and conflict between the two, mitigated by corruption of Parliament by the Crown, was the keynote of the constitutional struggles of the 17th century, which ended in the downfall of the Stuart line. The first two Hanoverian Kings, who succeeded the Stuarts, were foreigners who knew no English and were mainly interested in their German dominions. The government of Great Britain they left to ministers who could control the House of Commons. George III, who knew English, and was more interested in his British than in his German dominions, tried to go back on this system. By wholesale corruption he endeavoured to make Parliament amenable to his will, and chose as his ministers, not the real popular leaders, but men who would stoop to be instruments of corruption. One result was the loss of America. The situation was saved by the fact that the Younger Pitt, the popular leader, gained a great ascendancy over the King, whose mind presently began to fail. The principle that the King must choose as his ministers men, who for the time being were able to command a majority in the legislature, was gradually established. The principle was finally confirmed with the advent to the throne of a girl Queen in 1837. Thenceforward the Sovereign was removed from the position of ruler to that of an hereditary President in a commonwealth. The power of the mediaeval Sovereign passed to the leaders, who, for the time being, were able to command a majority in Parliament. This command of the legislature was the condition of office. *Responsible government is simply a means of securing that the Executive can control the legislature, the necessary condition of all government.*

The history of constitutional government in Scotland, Ireland and the Colonies enforces the same lesson.

The Scottish Parliament first came into effective being in the struggle with the Stuarts. The crisis began when, in 1693, the Scottish Parliament passed a Bill fatal to the monopoly of the English East India Company. Tweedale, the King's minister, yielding to his feelings as a Scottish nationalist, disobeyed the orders of William III and ratified the Bill. Serious complications with Spain were the result, and finally the financial ruin of Scotland. The efforts made to render the system workable by corruption broke down. Nationalist feeling was too strong for such expedients. The crisis was precipitated in 1701, when the Scottish Parliament refused to pass a Bill providing that on the death of Queen Anne, the same King should succeed to the Scottish as to the English throne.

Separation and war were avoided by the merging of the English and Scottish Parliaments in one Parliament of Great Britain. The problem of securing harmony between the legislatures and executives in both countries was thus consolidated and transferred to Westminster to find its solution there a century later.

The very same problem was provoked by the Irish Parliament in the reign of Henry VII. The problem was partly solved by Poyning's law, which deprived the Irish Parliament of all power of initiative. Many other causes were operating to prevent the establishment of order in Ireland. The system, such as it was,

was worked by open corruption. For value paid in titles, patronage and coin certain powerful families, called the "Undertakers," made themselves responsible for obtaining in the legislature the majorities required by the Irish executive. But again nationalist feeling was too strong for corruption. In 1782, in the throes of the American War, Poyning's law was repealed, and Ireland was given a constitution strictly comparable with that which is now proposed for India. Corruption was worked to the full; but government atrophied, till, in 1798, Ireland was a scene of weltering chaos and bloodshed The remedy was found by merging the Irish in the British Parliament. The difficulty of granting Home Rule to Ireland to-day largely has its roots in the anarchy which prevailed throughout the 18th century.

In the American colonies the same system obtained from the outset. The Executives could not obtain the laws necessary to secure order between the colonists and the Indians, nor yet the revenues needed for purely American purposes. The result was the revolution and secession of the colonies. The position had then to be faced by Washington. The basic elements of American society were drawn from the most law-abiding classes in England. But Washington found that he was dealing with a society which had grown unused to the restraints of any government whatever. Implored to use his great influence to restore order in Massachusetts, he replied with the memorable aphorism "Influence is not government." Charged with the task of creating an American Government, he solved the problem by making the Executive and legislature amenable to the same electorate. In a rigid and imperfect manner he anticipated the great discovery of responsible government, which had yet to be made in England.

The same features as had vitiated the American system were reproduced under the Quebec Act in the Provinces of Upper and Lower Canada. The legislatures were elective, while the executives, though mainly if not entirely consisting of Canadians, were appointed from England. Chronic and increasing friction were the result, leading to deadlock, and ending in the third decade of the 19th century in two rebellions, one in each Province. Lord Durham was then sent out, and produced a report on the whole situation, which first explained to Englishmen the nature of the great discovery they had made at home —responsible government. Durham recommended its application to Canada. He pointed out that no executive can continue to discharge its functions unless it can control the legislature. This, however, was impossible where, as in Canada, the mainspring of the Executive was in London, while the mainspring of the legislature was in Canada. The Imperial Government must either abolish the elective principle in the legislature, and so make it subordinate to the Executive, or else place the Executive in the hands of the leaders who controlled the legislature for the time being. The power of the Executive to carry laws, money and otherwise, essential to the maintenance of the Queen's government, was an absolute necessity. His advice was taken, and applied, not only to Canada, but also to other parts of the British Commonwealth, wherever the material for adequate electorates already existed.

The system condemned by Durham was recently revived in the case of the Transvaal in the Lyttelton constitution of 1906. The files of *Hasard* are not accessible, but I venture to suggest that, if any one will search them, he will find that the case urged against that measure by the Liberal opposition rests on the considerations adduced in this memorandum. That constitution never came into force; but, had it done so, no one, in the light of after events, can doubt that it would have come to a deadlock in the first session. The Appropriation Bill would never have been passed, and the Governor would have been faced with the same situation as confronted Durham in Canada.

In all these cases, be it noted, the materials for electorates existed already. These struggles were not, in fact, the exercise which fitted electorates for responsible government. Rather they resulted from communities already fit for self-government, who were feeling about in the darkness, until they discovered by trial, failure, and retrial the mechanism whereby the action of the Executive and legislature could be harmonised on the basis of popular government. The lesson of these blunders can be read. There is nothing to be gained by repeating them in a country like India, but infinite peril by reason of the irritation they cause.

The experience gained on this subject in various parts of the British Commonwealth is ably reviewed by A. Lawrence Lowell, the President of Harvard University, in the second volume of his standard work, *The Government of England*, which is, by the way, on the syllabus of the Calcutta University. He then goes on to examine two cases in which the Imperial Government, having advanced along the lines now proposed in India, had to go back instead of advancing to responsible government.

THE CROWN COLONIES.

> * The old system of a governor appointed by the Crown coupled with a legislature elected by the people has disappeared also in most of the colonies whose inhabitants are not mainly of European origin, but in this case the evolution has proceeded in the opposite direction. And here it may be observed that in some colonies where the population was white a hundred years ago, it is no longer so now; not in consequence of any great change in the proportion of the races, but because however numerous the slaves might be, they were, until freed, of no political account. In this way most of the British West Indies, where formerly the Europeans were almost alone considered, are now filled with a teeming free population, of which the whites form a very small part.
>
> The history of Jamaica may serve to illustrate the transformations by which the earlier form of government has been turned into that of a modern crown colony. Captured from the Spaniards in 1655, the island was

* "The Government of England," by A. Lawrence Lowell, volume II, Chapter LVI.

rapidly settled by Englishmen, and Lord Windsor, on his appointment as Governor in 1662, was instructed to call legislative assemblies according to the custom of the other colonies. Thus a government of the familiar type was created, with a royal governor, an appointed council, and an elected assembly. A score of years had not passed before friction with England began, and although in this instance matters were soon adjusted, troubles arose again later, and throughout the eighteenth century we find in a milder form quarrels, of the same nature as in the North American Colonies, constantly breaking out between the Governor and the Assembly. That body refused for years to vote a permanent revenue, and made appropriations to be expended only by officers appointed by itself. In fact, by a series of local acts the collection and expenditure of the revenue was taken almost entirely out of the hands of the Governor, and transferred to commissioners who were really the members of the Assembly under another name. Had the island been inhabited only by Englishmen, these difficulties might eventually have led, as in Canada, to the grant of a responsible ministry, but the presence of slaves, ten times as numerous as the free whites, led in the nineteenth century to both economic and political upheavals.

In 1807 Parliament forbade the slave trade, and this caused a scarcity of labour in Jamaica. In 1833 it went much further and against a protest of the Assembly denying its right to interfere in the internal affairs of the island, it abolished slavery, granting to the planters a compensation which they regarded as wholly inadequate. As the negroes in that climate could easily get a living from unoccupied lands without working for wages, emancipation struck a severe blow at the industries of the colony. In 1838 Parliament again undertook to legislate about the domestic concerns of the island; this time by an Act which took the regulation of prisons out of the hands of the local authorities. Whereupon the Assembly, in consideration of "the aggressions which the British Paliament continue to make on the rights of the people" of the colony, resolved to "abstain from any legislative function except such as may be necessary to preserve inviolate the faith of the island with the public creditor." The English ministry then brought in a bill to suspend the constitution of Jamaica. This, however, was defeated in the House of Commons, causing the fall of Lord

Melbourne's cabinet, and although Sir Robert Peel failed to form a ministry on account of the famous "Bedchamber Question," Melbourne on returning to power made no second attempt to pass the bill.

The planters must have felt that England was hounding them to their ruin, for in 1848 the foundations of their former prosperity were undermined still further by the adoption of free trade, and the removal of preferential tariffs in favour of sugarfrom the British West Indies. The Assembly, under the pressure of economic distress, passed retrenchment bills, which the appointed Council rejected as a breach of public faith, and the deadlock continued until, by the offer of a loan of half a million pounds, the Assembly was induced in 1854 to consent to a revision of its fundamental laws. The new constitution of that year enlarged the powers of the Governor in various ways; among others by transferring to him the functions hitherto exercised by the members of the Assembly when acting as commissioners for collecting and expending the revenue; and although he was to be assisted in the performance of his duties by an Executive Committee composed of three members of the Assembly and one of the Council, those members were to be selected by him.

For half a dozen years the new machinery worked well enough, but the opportunity for political deadlocks had by no means been removed, and in 1860 strife between the Governor and the Assembly began afresh. The first occasion thereof was a question about the responsibility of the Executive Committee for an over-expenditure; but the quarrel, as often happens, wandered off into other paths, and might have continued merrily on its way had not an alarming insurrection of the negroes broken out in 1865. Governor Eyre was accused of cruelty in suppressing it, but his action, which was vigorous and decisive, won the admiration of the white people. They had, in fact, been thoroughly frightened, and were ready to surrender their political rights for the sake of having a strong executive. At the close of 1866, therefore, the legislature of Jamaica authorised the Queen to create a new government for the island, and by an Act of Parliament the elective Assembly, after a life of two hundred years, came to an end.

Under the constitution which went into effect in 1867, the island become a crown colony with a single

Legislative Council, composed of six unofficial members, all appointed by the Crown The former were the principal officers of state in the island, such as the Colonial Secretary, the Attorney-General and the Commauder of the troops, while the Governor himself acted as chairman. But the political experiments in Jamaica were not yet over. After a few years the planters recovered from their fright, and longed to have the administration of public affairs once more in their own hands. In 1876, they sent a memorial to the House of Commons, asking that the inhabitants might have representatives in the Council and might control the revenues. The Secretary of State replied that a suggestion to alter the constitution so recently established could not be entertained. But when similar petitions were made in later years, the government yielded to the extent of permitting half of the seats in the Council to be elective. The change was made by the Constitution of 1884, whereby the Council was to consist of the Governor, and of nine appointed, and nine elected, members. Inasmuch as the Governor could control the appointed members, such an arrangement would appear to place a constant majority at his command, but this result was modified by a provision that a two-thirds vote of the elective members on financial questions, or a unanimous vote of those members on any other subject, should be decisive, unless the Governor considered the matter of paramount public importance. In other words, he had power to override the elected members, but he was not intended to use that power for current affairs.

Except for a few changes that do not concern us here, the Constitution of 1884 remained unaltered until 1897, when the Council was enlarged in a way which must be described in order to make clear the present method of controlling that body. The elected members were increased from nine to fourteen, one for each of the parishes in the island. At the same time the official and appointed members were raised only to ten, or, including the Governor, to eleven, but he was empowered to add four more if a question of great importance made it necessary to do so. In short, he was normally in a minority in the Council, but as a last resort could transform his appointees into a majority. This he did a couple of years later, after a long series of altercations with the elected members, chiefly on the subject of the taxes.

For some time insular finance had been perplexing. There had been deficits, and the Governor with the appointed members felt that the revenue must be made to balance the expenditure; while the elected members, suffering under the weight of the existing taxation, were loath to increase their burdens. Finally, in 1899, the Governor proposed a tax on typewriters, sewing machines, books and magazines, and when the elected members refused to vote for it, he made appointments to the four additional seats on the Council. The step was taken after a consultation with Mr. Chamberlain, then Secretary of State for the Colonies, and although the additional members resigned soon afterwards, on an undertaking by the elective councillors to vote for the tax, their appointment showed that the home government were prepared in cases of serious disagreement to exert its authority by overpowering the elective element in the Council.

The history of Jamaica is the more instructive, because the government in its transition from the old type to its present form has passed through an unusual variety of metamorphoses. It has had alongside of the Governor an Assembly wholly elected, a single Legislative Council wholly appointed, and a Council in which the elected members were, or could be made, a minority. Each of these forms is still found in the crown colonies, but save in a very few cases the first of them has disappeared and the prevalent types are those in which the legislature is composed exclusively, or for the major part, of appointed members.

A more recent example of the tendency to do away with an elective assembly, where full responsible government cannot be granted, may be seen in the case of Malta. After its captnre from the French in 1800 the island was at first under the sole authority of a Governor, who was often the Commander-in-Chief of the forces there; and in fact it is the great importance of Malta as a naval base that has prevented it from acquiring any large measure of self-government. Strategic considerations will not permit the people to govern themselves as they please, and yet the inhabitants, who enjoyed a representative assembly before the coming of the Knights of St. John, are so numerous that the post cannot be treated, like Gibraltar, simply as a garrison. But this peculiar condition, which has precluded government by responsible ministry on one side, and pure military rule on the other, does not make the political events in the island less valuable as an illustration of the difficulty of maintaining a semi-popular form of administration.

An advisory council was associated with the government of Malta in 1838-39, but no trace of popular representation was introduced until 1849, when the Crown by Letters Patent created a Council of Government, composed of the Governor with nine appointed, and eight elective, members. This gave the people of the island a chance to make their opinions heard, but not to make them prevail, for the government always had a majority at its command, and at times used it so freely as to foster a strong desire to bring the local administration under real popular control. The agitation continued for many years, and finally a plan for a new Council, based upon petitions by the Maltese themselves, was put into effect by Letters Patent of 1887. It reduced the appointed members to six, and increased the elected ones to fourteen, of whom ten were chosen by the ordinary voters, while the clergy, the nobility, the graduates of the university and the chamber of commerce had one representative apiece. Thus the elected members preponderated heavily, and, what is more, on money bills their votes alone were to be counted. On the other hand, the Crown had not only the usual veto and an exclusive right to initiate measures dealing with the revenue, but reserved to itself an ultimate power to legislate ndependently by Order in Council.

The Maltese soon found that their actual control over the government was less than they had expected, and as early as 1891, after the elected members had resigned as a protest against the policy of the Governor, a riot was caused by the attempt of a mob to overawe the Council. Dissensions continued, with resignation as an occasional resource, but the popular party had no specific issue as a basis for opposition until 1898. In that year Colonel Hewson, a British army officer, who had given evidence in English as a witness, and was asked to sign a translation of it into Italian, the official language of the court, refused to do so on the ground that he could not read what he was required to sign. Thereupon he was committed for contempt of court; and although the Governor saved him from going to gaol, indignation was felt that a British officer should be ordered to prison by a British court for refusing to sign a statement in a foreign tongue that he did not understand. Mr. Chamberlain directed the Governor to lay before the Council ordinances making English as well as Italian the official language of the courts, and when the Council rejected them, they were enacted by Order in Council in March 1899. The elected members protested, resigned, were returned again without opposition, and then refused to pass money bills, which were in turn put in force by Order in Council.

The question of language involved a singular state of affairs. Italian, which had been substituted for Latin in the courts after the English occupation, was the tongue of the educated classes, but not of the great mass of the population, who speak Maltese, a dialect based upon Arabic. It could fairly be asserted, therefore, that English was quite as appropriate an official language as Italian. The question affected the schools as well as the courts.

Some time before a plan had been put in force whereby the children were taught Maltese in the two youngest classes, and then the parents were allowed to choose whether they should study English or Italian, with the result that by far the greater part of them chose the former. But now the elected members of the Council, claiming that the voice of the parents was not really free, demanded that Italian should be the regular subject of study, and declined to pass some of the appropriations for the schools unless an ordinance for the purpose was adopted. In an interview with Mr. Chamberlain their delegates went much further, asking for responsible government. Such a request was of course refused, with an intimation that the elected members did not fairly represent the people of the colony; and in view of the small proportion of voters and the still smaller number who went to the polls, this may very well have been true.

The leaders of the opposition to the government set on foot a vigorous agitation in the island; while in the Council they passed their ordinance for the schools; only to see it met by a veto. Thereupon they rejected appropriation, resigned, and were again re-elected. Clearly the constitution as it stood did not work. The popular element was too strong or too weak to please any one; and finally in 1903 the gordian knot was cut by Letters Patent which abolished the Council, and substituted another composed, in addition to the Governor, of ten appointed, and only eight elected, members. The Governor was given also the sole right of initiating measures, and thus the Council was reduced to a consultative body where the representatives of the people can express their opinions, but have no means of putting them into effect. After an experience of seventeen years the Constitution of 1887 had been abandoned, and the conditions of 1849 have been restored. Nor was the result due to a change of party in England, for the Letters Patent of 1887 had been issued by a Conservative ministry. *The constitution of that year was doomed to fail, because it created two independent forces that were almost certain to come into collision, without any power which could bring them into harmony. Parliamentary government avoids deadlock by making the executive responsible to the legislature. Presidential government limits deadlocks, because all the organs of the state must ultimately submit to a superior tribunal, the electorate of the nation. But a legislature elected by the people coupled with a Governor appointed by a distant power, is a contrivance for fomenting dissensions and making them perpetual.*

Such being the experience of the British Commonwealth, as interpreted by an American investigator of the highest authority, advocates of this principle are commonly driven to defend it by appealing to the examples of Germany and Austria. Mr. Gokhale, for instance, advises that "The relations of the Executive "Government and the Legislative Councils so constituted should be roughly similar to those between the "Imperial Government and the Reichstag in Germany." Before, however, we accept German guidance in the task of extending self-government to India, it is well to examine a little more closely, than I think Mr. Gokhale had done, the inner working of the elective institutions which the monarchs of Central Europe have used as a mask for despotism. Some years ago I had an informing conversation on this subject with the correspondent of the *Frankfurter Zeitung*, which was then an organ of German liberalism. "How is "it," I asked, "that your Emperor is able to pass "his budgets and measures through an assembly based "on male adult suffrage?" "Because," my German "friend replied, "whenever the Reichstag has rejected "measures which the Emperor deems essential, the "Emperor has dissolved them, and appealed to the "nation to support him. And so far the nation has "always given the Emperor the majority for which he "has asked." "Do you mean," I enquired, "that "your Emperor goes electioneering, and that the voters "support him against their own representatives?" "That is what it comes to," he said. "You, of "course, do not understand the power which the "Kaiser's claim to divine right still has over the minds "of the German people, a power reinforced by an un-"broken chain of military success for the last century." "But this claim to superior wisdom based on divine "right," I objected, "will scarcely continue to prevail "indefinitely with an educated people like the Germans. "Sooner or later the voters will refuse to listen to the "Kaiser's appeal, and will support their own represen-"tatives by returning a majority pledged to reject the "Emperor's measures." My friend threw up his hands "in horror and cried, "God forbid! We should then "lose our constitution. The Emperor would simply "dismiss the Reichstag, collect the taxes and proceed "to administer the country without them, with the "army at his back." "But the army," I urged, "is "the nation in arms. Why do you fear that the nation "in arms should support the Emperor against the nation "at the ballot box?" "It is just the habit of military "discipline," he replied. "So long as the German "people are dazzled by a course of unbroken military "success, the prestige of the monarchy will remain un-"impaired and all powerful. The power of the head of "the army over the soldiers will be stronger than the "spirit of freedom amongst those soldiers in private "life." From that moment onwards I felt that war was inevitable. If the system rested on the military prestige of the dynasty, and the habit of blind obedience in the ranks, that habit would have to be exercised in war, and the prestige of the dynasty would have to be refreshed with new victories. And now, when the failure of the Kaiser's brutal designs is casting its shadow on the dynasty's prestige, the Reichstag is beginning to assert its claim to make and unmake the Executive. To that claim the Kaiser is opposing his own, that his ministers are responsible to him alone, as he himself is responsible, not to the people of Germany, but to God. The system cannot outlast the failure and fall of the Prussian autocracy. Reformers will be wise to look for some other model upon which to base the first steps towards responsible government in India.

Outside the British Commonwealth a number of countries have endeavoured to pass from paternal to popular government. Of these I can only think of two important cases in which the transition has been effected without a long series of revolutions and civil disorders. These two are Italy and Japan. The nucleus of modern Italy was Piedmont, a state in which constitutional government had already been achieved. In both these cases the transition was watched and tended by native monarchs who, unlike the German Emperor, used their personal prestige to guide the nation from paternal to popular government. Mr. Price Collier states that on several occasions, when the opposition in the Japanese Assembly threatened to embarrass the Government, a message was sent to them from the Mikado that their speeches disturbed the souls of his ancestors. Instantly the opposition collapsed. In plain words the Mikado, in guiding his people towards responsible government, made full use of the religious veneration with which his throne was regarded. In India an alien Government has no such appeal to make. Still less can it go on election campaigns like the German Emperor.

Elsewhere the movement towards responsible government has proceeded through a series of violent and bloody disorders. France, Mexico, the South American Republics, Turkey, Persia, China and Russia are cases in point. Not all of these countries can be said to have yet reached the goal of responsible government; and the failure has been most marked, whereever the country was so large that it was necessary to organize Provincial democracies as well as a central democracy, and bring these different organs of Government into proper relation with each other. The reason for the success achieved in America and the British Dominions was in great measure due to the fact that the provincial democracies were thoroughly developed and established before any attempt was made to bring the central government under popular control.

VI

ALTERNATIVE METHODS COMPARED.

Imperial, and even provincial, executives are somewhat removed from the facts to which their decisions relate. The springs of action may be weakened at headquarters some time before the effects are seen in the field. A poison may be none the less deadly because it is slow, but the connection of cause and effect are harder to trace. It is perilously easy for one generation to ignore the results of a system which will only mature in the time of their successors. But when in 1912 Mr. Gokhale proposed to extend the principle, already applied to the Indian and Provincial Executives, to the District Executive, Lord Hardinge's Government were quick to see where it led. Speaking on behalf of that Government, the Member for the Home Department reviewed that proposal as follows:—

> "Well, Sir, as the Hon'ble Mover has said, he only wishes this Council to be advisory to *begin with*. This council of nine men when we come to look to Mr. Gokhale's proposals we find that so far from being advisory to begin with, they are very largely administrative councils, and that is the view which has been taken by many Hon'ble Members of this Council—they want not advisory but administrative or executive councils. Well, Sir, I have said enough to show that Collectors and executive officers will not be rendered more efficient by a council of this kind; but that if local matters are to be referred to anybody, it must be local bodies and that the hopes lie with them; but in case this Council desire to pass this resolution in agreement with the Hon'ble Mr. Gokhale, I should like it to feel not only that this Collector's council might be *to begin with*, but what it might become to end with. I fear myself that the nine councillors intended by the Hon'ble Mr. Gokhale as nine muses to inspire the Collector, would end by becoming nine millstones round his neck. If that should come to pass, we might as well do away

with the unfortunate Collector altogether. Now, Sir, the Hon'ble Mr. Gokhale has not repeated what he has said in his evidence before the Decentralisation Commission, and it may perhaps interest you to know before you agree to his council of nine. Under his scheme you would already have succeeded in abolishing the post of Commissioner, and there would be no one left beween the Local Government and the Collector.

"If I have been able to convince Hon'ble Members here that the Collector would also go, I should very much like to know what the opinion of the Council will be. I hardly suppose that the Hon'ble Mover himself contemplates this result absolutely with equanimity. I do not think that the Council will do so either, and I am perfectly sure that any such idea as the elimination of the Collector or the emasculation of his power would be viewed with the utmost consternation and concern by the masses of the people, to whom the impartiality of the Collector, and, I may add, his independence, is the very sheet anchor of their trust in British administration. As far as Government is concerned, I can only say that if this proposal, as devised by the Hon'ble Mr. Gokhale, were carried out and carried to its logical conclusions, it would undermine the executive power of the Government, and it is quite impossible therefore that the Government of this country can contemplate for a moment its executive powers being undermined."

The general teaching of experience needs to be studied to the full. But the real intrinsic nature of the problem before us has to be grasped, and a new solution devised to fit its peculiar conditions. We shall not solve it by tearing leaves wholesale out of the records of precedents. We must think for ourselves, and have the courage to add a new page to the volume of human experience. The root of the problem, I suggest, is to bring electorates, however small, into being; to give them genuine responsibilities; to enable them to trace the effect of the votes they give on their own lives and so to connect cause and effect; to watch the results; and to add responsibilities with a generous hand, as fast as the results justify the addition, at the same time increasing the electorates as rapidly as may be.

It is in the light of this conception that I propose to examine the one expedient which I have so far seen proposed which does not proceeed upon the principle of leaving the Executives responsible to Parliament in England, while making them dependent for their powers on elective assemblies in India, unweighted by any responsibility for seeing that the government is carried on. The plan in question is to institute complete responsible government in one selected area and observe the results. Underlying this suggestion is, I feel, the fallacious assumption that communities being either fit or unfit for self-government, statesmanship, therefore, consists in discovering to which of two categories a given community belongs. Now India is of all countries the most diverse, not only in race, language and religion, but also in the degree of advancement attained by its various parts. One test of one part would be little or no criterion of the others. Moreover, the institution of full responsible government in one province only would tend to make the others unmanageable. Men are sentient beings; and you cannot import the methods of a physical laboratory into political research. The general unrest produced throughout the rest of India, which was asked to wait indefinitely, would react on the favoured province, and prejudice the results of the experiment there. If the first experiments on responsible government are to succeed, it must be in an India at peace in her own mind and throughout her coasts.

This expedient, moreover, mistakes the whole character of the problem, as I see it, which is to train electorates throughout India by the exercise of real responsibilities proportioned to the strength of the electorate for the time being. The process of education should proceed simultaneously in all parts of British India, according to the pace at which each community is able to move. The example set by the more advanced communities will be simply invaluable, but only if the more backward communities are given the opportunity of emulating and imitating that example at once, so far as in them lies. They must be allowed to feel that the successful exercise of one power will quickly be followed by the addition of others.

This particular proposal has been mooted by men who are just as firmly convinced as I am that responsible government is the only sound goal of policy, and are no less anxious to reach it. On several occasions, however, I have met people who honestly believed that the goal of self-government for India was a mirage, and have done their best to convert me to that view. Such people are fertile in negative advice. Having listened to the reasons against every suggested course, I have always made a point of asking them what positive suggestion they would offer, assuming that public opinion in England insists that something should be done. Pressed to this point, the advice of such men has usually been to initiate full responsible government in one province as an experiment. That, they believe, would convince public opinion at home of the truth of their own conviction that responsible government is a goal of policy impossible for India. I agree that the results of so drastic an experiment would be likely to fail. But the failure would lead to a wholly misleading conclusion. You might just as well set out to test the potential vitality of a man long bed-ridden, by sending him to march twenty miles the first day. The proper course is to develop his strength by a little exercise gradually increased as the patient can bear it. That I submit can only be done by transferring some genuine functions to Indian executives responsible to electorates, and by increasing the burden as each of them shows its capacity to carry more.

VII

THE GOAL.

The principle of specific delegation is highly elastic. It admits of infinite diversity of application. To begin with, it involves a reconsideration of the map. But that is a virtue rather than a defect; for, if anything is certain, it is this, that a map of India designed from first to last to suit the needs of a highly bureaucratic government, with its mainspring in England, is not suited to a country governed by Executives responsible to electorates in India itself: and that is the goal to which we are now pledged. Every step we now take, and specially the first, must look to a time when all purely Indian questions will be decided in India by Indian electorates. We are bound to test all our proposals by the question how they will lead to that goal, and, when it is reached, how far they will harmonize with its conditions. The very object of stating a goal is to avoid makeshifts, which come to stay, and hang about the neck of the future like millstones. It is capacity to work with an eye on the distant goal, which distinguishes the statesman from mere politicians who live from hand to mouth.

Now what are purely Indian questions? To answer that question we must ask another—what is India? The goal of responsible government implies an ideal inseparable from its attainment—a self-governing nation or nations, a Dominion or Dominions within the limits of the British Commonwealth. Now is India to be the future home of one nation, or a group of nations; of one Dominion, or of a group of Dominions? To bring matters down to a fine point, is Europe the model upon which India is to develop, or rather is she to seek her example in the territories covered by the United States of America? There are two schools of thought on this subject, and it is essential that the issues between them should be thought out in time. For everything which follows will depend upon which of those two conceptions are chosen.

The great diversity of India in respect of race, language and religion, points to Europe rather than the United States as the natural model to be followed. If so, our aim will then be to mould Bengal, Madras, Bombay, the Punjab, the United Provinces, and the other existing provinces of India into nations, each with a domestic government responsible to itself. But if we are really keeping the goal of responsible government in our minds, this conception breaks down at the outset. We are bound to look at future needs, as well as at present conditions. These units, large as they are, have common interests which are strictly Indian, railways, tariffs, social law and commercial law, which cannot be controlled by these units acting apart. The recent experience of South Africa, and the older experience of the other Dominions, and of the United States, proves that a number of self-governing units cannot control these interests, without establishing a central government responsible to all the communities alike. Unless we look forward to an Indian Government responsible to the whole people of India for the control of interests too large for any of her provinces, those interests will have to be controlled by the Imperial Government from outside. That is the view expressed in Lord Islington's recent lecture at Oxford, but it is utterly incompatible with the Pronouncement of the 20th of August. If Indian tariffs are always to be controlled by the Imperial Government, then matters which are strictly Indian will be controlled by an authority outside India, and that is the negation of responsible government. The nations of Europe, with all their diversity, have such interests in common, interests which cannot be controlled, so long as they remain divided in separate camps, with no common authority and no common law. Hence the spectre of war, which the United States has long banished from her shores, haunts, and will long continue to haunt, Europe. Unless India is doomed to the fate of Europe, her common interests must be controlled.

We are pledged to the goal of transferring that control to India herself. Responsible government means no less, and it is in realizing that control, in becoming the mistress of her own house and in all its chambers, that India will transcend the diversity of her races, religions and tongues, and attain in the end to the consciousness of nationalism and to the verity of nationhood. The recent declaration leaves us no choice. It is not Europe which we can take as the model for India, but a super-nation, conceived on the scale of the United States of America, as that nation would have been, had it remained within the precincts of the British Commonwealth.

This conception, which we cannot evade, without being false to our pledges, brings with it the motive, in the absence of which all schemes of self-government, all projects of making a nation in India, will fail. The ideal of an Indian nation, the appeal of Indian patriotism, is the choice which educated Indians themselves will make. The appeal of a Bengali nation, or of a Punjabi nation, is not of itself large enough to evoke the spirit of devotion upon which alone self-government can rest. It was love of Japan which moved her people to seek from all the world the knowledge which might raise their country to the plane achieved by other great nations of the world. This devotion to a great country, existing or to be, is the spiritual force without which education degenerates into mere instruction. If we do but think what the task of an English schoolmaster would be, could he never appeal to a sense of English nationalism, we shall realize this truth. As the name of England stirs ourselves, so must the name of India be brought to stir the children of this country. Personally I see in India little trace of spontaneous devotion to the British Commonwealth, or of Imperial patriotism as I conceive it,—the kind of sentiment which makes Australians and Canadians feel they would die sooner than see this Commonwealth perish, or their own nation cease to be part of it. Roots from which this greater love has sprung have yet to be planted in

India, and we must not look to gather that rich harvest, until the seeds of freedom have long flourished in her soil. Some gratitude exists in the minds of those who realize the benefits of British rule. Much loyalty there is on the part of princes and nobles to the person of the King. The legend of that King ruling a quarter of mankind has its hold on the oriental imagination of the dumb millions of the Indian mofussil. But those strong though delicate ties of mutual esteem and affection, by which the citizens of a true Commonwealth are knit, have yet to be developed. They will spring in time from the new policy. Their growth will be the triumph of a later age. For the present I believe there is nothing to be gained by artificial forcing of an Imperial patriotism, until a true Indian patriotism has become conscious in the life and soul of this people. Cultivate that; give it scope for expression, and above all a field for exercise; and one day the greater love of the greater Commonwealth will be found to have come without observation. With educated Indians this may be sooner than we now dream, if they be but given their place in the supreme councils of this world Commonwealth, to which they are entitled, and from which, indeed, they cannot be spared.

VIII

THE MAP OF INDIA.

It is in assuming the control of Indian affairs that an Indian patriotism and its after-fruits will develop. And no vision smaller than India will give to her people the internal driving force they need. Let us face the ideal of a united India in all its magnitude and in all its diversity. Let us face the difficulties with which that magnitude and diversity confront us, and endeavour to reduce them at the outset so far as we can. What place, for instance, has Burma in the vision of a future Indian nation? Geographically she is as far removed from India as Rangoon is from Calcutta. In race, language and religion, her people have scarcely a point in common with those of India. The attempt to incorporate Burma in the fabric of Indian administration is the consequence of a system, the antithesis of popular government, which groups different communities without reference to anything but immediate administrative convenience. Burma was incorporated in India when our policy was dominated by the conception of a vast Eastern dependency. That conception is now abandoned, and India and Burma ought to be divorced. The people of neither country desire the alliance. The Burmese member has no proper place in the Indian legislature. If we really intend to create a united self-governing India, Burma should be emancipated from the Government of India, and should either be placed under the personal rule of the Viceroy, or its Government should be rendered answerable to the Secretary of State for India direct It will be more contrary to nature to force Burma into the fabric of an Indian nationhood, than to incorporate Ireland in Great Britain, or Finland in Russia. To this important extent the problem can be simplified at once.

India, we have said, must come to control affairs

which are purely Indian. She is however to remain an integral part of the British Commonwealth. Her foreign affairs are those of the whole Commonwealth. She can never therefore control them apart. They form an integral part of the foreign affairs of the whole Commonwealth, in the control of which she must come to share. The Indian frontier is a large item in foreign affairs. Live wires run from it throughout the whole of Asia and Europe, the mismanagement of which at this end may involve the whole Commonwealth in war and set the whole of the world on fire. Here is the one critical frontier in any part of the British Dominions, and, if India were now inhabited by a people already as fitted and practised in self-government as those of England herself, it would not be possible, so long as they remain part of the British Commonwealth, to place the Indian frontier under the control of a Government responsible only to the people of India. That frontier must remain under the sole, unfettered control of the Imperial Government charged with the conduct of foreign affairs. This principle ought to be enunciated and implemented now, and effect can only be given to it by reserving from the outset a strip, however narrow, from sea to sea, which would isolate a self-governing India from any contact with foreign frontiers. The proposal means no more than completing the policy inaugurated by Lord Curzon when he separated the North-West Frontier Province from the Punjab. That province has simply to be extended down the right bank of the Indus to the Arabian Sea, and eastwards along the foothills of the mountain barrier, taking a narrow strip not more than a few miles wide along the frontiers of Nepal, to the point where the boundaries of India and Burma meet on the confines of Tibet. The self-governing India of the future would then be as well isolated from complications with foreign powers as Australia herself. The future destination of the frontier province would be signalized by removing it to the personal control of the Viceroy from the jurisdiction of the Governor-General in Council, the members of which are destined to become hereafter the ministers of a cabinet responsible to an Indian Parliament. This arrangement would be closely analogous to that under which the Governor-General of South Africa is, in that capacity, the legal head of the Union Government, while, as High Commissioner, he is responsible to the Secretary of State for the Colonies, as *de facto* ruler of all British South African territories not included in the Union.

If once it were understood that India were to be separated from foreign complications by a province destined to remain subject to the Imperial Government as absolutely and as finally as Malta or Gibraltar, the whole project of developing India as a self-governing Dominion will begin to assume a different aspect. A large factor in the alarm, with which the cautious Englishman views that prospect, arises from the half-conscious dread in the back of his mind as to what would happen to the peace of the whole Commonwealth, if this, its one critical frontier, were relegated to the charge of a Dominion ministry. Such a thing would be utterly wrong in principle. Imperial control of the frontier ought to be established from the outset, and, when once that has been definitely settled, the Imperial Government can embark on steps for establishing India on the same footing as the self-governing Dominions with a lighter heart and a clearer mind.

The territory, then, of which I am thinking as the home of a future self-governing Dominion is the Indian Peninsula bounded by the Indus, the line where the plains meet the Himalayan range and the line which divides Burma from Assam and Bengal. It is to this territory that we should consider how we are going to apply the conception of a supernation organized on the lines of the United States of America, as it would have been, had it developed as a self-governing Dominion of the British Commonwealth. Let us think how this conception affects the internal structure of the map. American publicists of the 18th century were accustomed to speak of the thirteen States as "these nations." The application of the word "nation" to any State of the American Union would be quite impossible to-day. An American thinks of the whole Republic as his nation, and the State has now been reduced to its proper level in his mind—to the level of a province. But the province is an essential organ of that vast polity. It was far too great ever to be ruled on the lines of self-government by one Administration from one centre. A nation so vast could only govern itself, provided that it was cut up into a number of provinces, each managing its own affairs for itself. These provinces had first to be got into working order on self-governing lines, with areas appropriate thereto. Then, and then only, could they be brought into proper relation to each other and to a central national Government charged with the conduct of all functions too large for the several provinces to control. Amongst the problems which distract Russia at this moment are those of finding areas appropriate to provincial self-government, of equipping them with electoral Governments of their own, of reconstituting the National Government on an electoral basis, of giving to each authority its appropriate functions and revenues, and of driving all these coaches through the gate of a revolution side by side. In India, happily, there is no need to court disaster by trying to do all these difficult things together in one operation.

With all the experience before us of America and the self-governing Dominions her map can be readjusted on lines compatible with the popular control of her institutions.

In guiding India from paternal to popular government one vital truth has always to be kept in mind. The areas and administrative mechanism developed by a system of paternal government, are utterly different from those developed by a system of popular government. When introducing responsible government in a great country which has never had it before, you must be prepared to revise your areas, and to reconstruct your administrative system. As every practical man knows, popular prejudice is always a factor which has to be considered in political arrangements. There is in human nature an element of conservatism which makes a great number of men cling to any arrangement to which they are accustomed. To a detached observer, one of the most pathetic features in the Indian situation is the tenacity with which certain elements of its people cling, and those the most vocal, to features in the system organized by us foreigners, which are in fact the greatest obstacles to popular government. One is our educational system; another is the Permanent Settlement; a third the vast satrapies into which our system has divided India. No statesman will disregard the prejudices of a highly conservative people in favour of the existing order. On the other hand no ruler will be worthy of the name of statesman who will not help Indians to escape from our arrangements, and from their own prejudice in favour of them, when to do so is necessary for the attainment of popular government in fact as well as in name. The tendency to act as though statesmanship consisted merely in listening to those living men who can make their voices heard is the curse of modern liberalism. It has been the undoing of Ireland, and may easily be that of India. Even where a people can speak with one united voice, their verdict may be fatal to after-generations, whose voice cannot as yet be heard. The duty of statesmen is to think out the plan which is right in itself, to state that plan clearly and boldly, and then guide the community towards it as closely as popular prejudice will allow, not failing to appeal to their innate sense of trusteeship for those who come after them.

I propose, therefore, to begin by considering what conditions, apart from popular prejudice, are needed to realize most quickly the scheme of responsible government for India outlined in the Pronouncement of the 20th of August. I shall then go on to suggest in what manner the people of India can best be helped to approximate to those conditions for themselves.

Now, looking at any great country, it is easy to see that there are certain areas correlative to certain organs of government. At the bottom you find the village, the town, and the district, so called in India, which corresponds to the English and American county or the French department. These areas are the field of what, in technical language, is called *local government*. In a later page we shall see how sharply the sphere of local government is to be distinguished from that of political government which belongs to provincial and national authorities. The one deals only with administrative detail, the other includes the settlement of wide political issues.

In all great communities the political field is, or ought to be, divided between one central government, and a number of provincial governments. There are various reasons for this, which can best be explained by keeping in mind the United States. Congress at Washington could not pass all the measures required by the different parts of that vast and varied community. It would break down for want of time, and its measures would not be sufficiently adapted to the needs of the various local communities. We cannot imagine one law and system of education for the whole of America. And, if we could, its administration from one centre would be too rigid. Areas so far removed as California and New York, need different systems, adapted to their local conditions and administered in response to the feelings of each community. Apart from this an educational system, administered from Washington for all America, would be too vast for any one authority to control.

These reasons for provincial governments and areas are sufficient; but they could be multiplied indefinitely. It is for want of such institutions that social reform is paralysed in the British Isles, France and Italy. One central government is unable to cope with the needs of thirty or forty millions. Effective social reform will never be attained, unless or until they develop self-governing Provinces commensurate with those of Switzerland, the Dominions, or the United States. The first problem before India is to get areas in which provincial self-government can be made effective.

At present the major self-governing provinces of India are as large as, or larger than, the three nations referred to above. How comes it that India is divided into units so vast?

Some light will be thrown on the question by a glance at the map of North America, as it existed in the middle of the 18th century. Its soil was then divided between three Great Empires, which all centred in Europe. Spain claimed to administer, as one huge province, all the territories now covered by Mexico, California, Arizona, New Mexico, Texas, Alabama and Florida. Similarly France claimed a vast triangular territory, of which the north-eastern angle was opposite Newfoundland, the north-western angle near Winnipeg, and the southern angle at the mouth of the Mississippi in the Gulf of Mexico. England claimed a much smaller area, the coast strip extending from the boundary which now divides New Brunswick and Maine to the northern boundary of Florida.

The vast territories of Spain and France were each governed as one great province from Mexico City and Quebec, respectively. The much smaller British strip was already, by the middle of the 18th century, partitioned into no less than thirteen self-governing colonies. This partition was the natural and necessary result of self-government. Now that the Spanish and French territories have all been brought under electoral government, they have all had to be subdivided in the same way. The lesson, which can be freely illustrated from Asia, is that centralised autocracies develop satrapies which are far too large for the purposes of provincial self-government. The old Chinese provinces are on far too large a scale for this purpose. Aggregates so vast include communities so various as to need different laws and institutions to suit their peculiarities. Provincial self-government has been evolved to meet this need. Quebec and Ontario were once placed under a single Government, which suited them ill; for one was Catholic, the other Protestant; one French, the other British. Roman law was the basis in one province, and English common law in the other. The creation of a federal government enabled them to develop as sub-nationalities of one great nation, like the English and Scots, and yet to be separated as self-governing provinces able to develop their respective institutions in harmony with their different conditions.

In Australia there were no such social, religious legal distinctions. The eastern coast belt was first organized as one Province of New South Wales, the whole of which was subject to the jurisdiction of the Governor at Sydney. But the moment popular institutions were introduced the settlers in the territories now known as Victoria and Queensland found themselves out in the cold, as compared with the central districts adjacent to Sydney. The community was too large for effective control under popular institutions. The result was that the electorates of Victoria and Queensland were both detached, and placed under separate Provincial Governments of their own.

If the areas of provincial self government are too large, an artificial and irksome unity is imposed upon the too widely different elements embraced, which presently demand to be sub-divided into smaller self-governing areas. Provinces, moreover, planned on the scale of nations tend to fall apart as separate national units. And besides all this, self-government, always a difficult business in its beginnings, is much more difficult, if first applied to a community so great that the various representatives know little of parts other than their own. To attempt self-government on too wide a scale is to prejudice its success at the outset.

All this has an obvious bearing on the existing Provinces of India. They are for the most part the artificial creations of a paternal and highly centralised Government which has its mainspring in England. They were designed as the satrapies of a vast oriental dependency. The United Provinces, for instance, contains 48,000,000, and is larger than any European state but the Russian and German Empires. It contains a large variety of languages, races and levels of society. To attempt the first essay in responsible government, by applying it to so vast and varied an aggregate, is to prejudice the whole experiment. It is also to court failure in the last stages of this great project of creating a united and self-governing India. These vast satrapies, conceived on the scale of considerable nations, will learn, under the influence of electoral government, to think as such, and so tend to fall apart, like the overgrown provinces of China. If India is to be taken as the true national unit, as it must be, it is of vital importance to consider now what the proper provincial units are to be, out of which the whole national fabric can be built. The moment you begin to establish electoral Governments, the boundaries of their jurisdictions, lightly sketched by the pencils of officials and diplomats, begin to bite into the political map like acids. The boundaries of artificial areas like those of Roumania, Bulgaria, and Serbia, carved out of the Turkish Empire, have within a few decades become lines over which their respective inhabitants have fought and bled. The internal peace of India generations hence will depend upon the wisdom and foresight with which the areas of provincial self-government are planned in the initial stages of the new departure.

Once again we may refer for guidance in solving this problem to the example of the United States of America. That Republic is divided into forty-eight states, with an average population of 2,000,000 souls. Of these the most closely settled is New York, with a population of 10,000,000. Thus, if we take the largest state of the United States of America as our standard, British India with its population of 240,000,000 might appropriately be divided into some twenty-four larger and smaller States. The term "States" was suggested to me as having two merits. In the first place it helps to suggest the model of the United States, and to keep it in mind. In the second place it gives a description nicely parallel to that of the Native States which might, I suggest, be conveniently described as 'Principalities.' This change of title will enable us to adopt the American term State in describing the provincial areas, which, as I think, India must have in a federal system based upon popular government. And in this connection let me add that the division of India into some twenty-four States would give areas far more comparable to the major Principalities, the largest of which, Hyderabad, contains 13,000,000 inhabitants. It is natural to suppose that the Princes of India will come to play a part in the life of the great nation to be called into being. If they follow the example set by several of the leading Princes, who have laid the foundations of a representative system, they will develop in the direction of consitutional monarchies, in sympathy with movement inaugurated in British India. The Princes themselves should be gathered in the Upper Chamber of a great Indian legislature, so that the Indian nation of the future will not lack the leadership, for which it will naturally look to its hereditary statesmen.

In suggesting the most populous state of the American Union with its population of 10,000,000, as the standard to be used for States in India, no suggestion is made that these States should be constituted on any mechanical principle. The defect of the present areas is that they are too mechanical. The province of Bihar and Orissa, for instance, combines communities with an almost cynical disregard of the differences between them. The plan suggested will remedy these unnatural unions. This particular province would fall naturally into three Provincial States—Bihar with its population of 24,000,000, and Orissa and Chota Nagpur with 5,000,000, apiece. But Orissa itself ought to be increased by the inclusion of those people of the same language and race who inhabit the northern extremity of Madras and the Central Province. The disparity in size between these areas is no greater than that which exists in the United States, and in all the other federal Unions. Bihar is of course a dangerously large unit upon which to begin an experiment in provincial self-government, and might have to be subdivided, as Virginia has been. The first consideration is to get communities which, as contrasted with those of the British Isles, France and Italy, are not too large for effective self-government on really provincial lines. Where possible, historic areas like Sind should be taken. But unity of language, race and religion are also important factors, and language is the most important of all. The greatest obstacle to a real extension of popular government in India is the practice of conducting public business in the English tongue. By all means let English occupy the same position as Hindustani has in Northern India, since the time of the Moghul Empire. In English lies the hope of National unity, and of knowledge from the outside world. Let the public records be kept in English; extend knowledge of that language in every possible direction. But if all discussion of public affairs is conducted in English, then public life is going to be confined for many generations to come to a narrowly restricted class. How can electorates ever be brought to grasp the questions submitted to their judgment, if all public discussion is to be conducted in a foreign tongue? The use of the vernaculars in politics is essential, if India is to advance towards responsible government at any but the slowest pace. The areas of Provincial self-government must be designed largely with a view to making it possible for public business to be discussed in a language which all the legislators can speak with ease, and which the largest possible number of electors can understand. Given these conditions, a vast number of landholders and others, who cannot conduct debates in English, are rendered available for public life. The hope of popular government lies in the vernaculars.*

The educated classes in India have long claimed their country's right to develop on the lines of a

---

* I had scarcely penned the above words when three Oriya gentlemen, who had just been attending a deputation to the Viceroy and Secretary of State, called to see me. Their attention had been caught by the treatment of the question of areas in the Joint Address, and they came to urge the necessity of basing self-government on racial and linguistic units. One part of the Oriya people are included in Madras and another in the Central Province. Naturally they desire a reunion with Orissa which will bring together, in one self-governing state, some 10,000,000 Oriya-speaking people.

self-governing Dominion, and that claim has now been recognized in words which I venture to prophesy will prove as irrevocable as Magna Charta itself. I have heard a number of Indians say that it is only in the last few months that they have begun to realize what responsible government means; and indeed it would be strange if it were otherwise. If Socrates were here he would say that such confessions were the beginning of wisdom, and if you are to take the self-governing Dominions as the model upon which you mean to construct the polity of India, it is vital to realize what a Dominion means. A community so different as India cannot copy their constitutions outright. The real lesson they have to teach is, that of all commonwealths, the polity of India must be built up by a series of experiments and in accordance with the lessons they give. But certain lessons can be learned at once, from the experience already gained by the Dominions, and one of those lessons can be read in Quebec. No one will question now that it was a mistake upon Durham's part to try to force this French people of the Roman Catholic communion into an unnatural union with the British and Protestant community of Ontario. The main point of the federal structure adopted by Canada is that it enables a national union to be realized, while leaving distinct racial, linguistic and religious units, organized as self-governing provinces, to lead their own life under their own conditions.

If this experience is held in mind, can we really look forward to a United States of India within the British Commonwealth, under which Sind and the Canarese-speaking people are tied and bound into the same self-governing unit as the Marathas? Are not the Marathas themselves entitled to a State such as will perpetuate the traditions of that famous community? Are the Tamil and Telugu peoples of Madras to be given no separate institutions of their own? Are the Oriyas to be left dispersed amongst three Provinces, the larger section being left under the permanent domination of the people of Bihar? To base responsible government on such units is not only to ignore the experience of the other Dominions, but to violate principles for which we are fighting in this war. You cannot base responsible government on units evolved on principles which are the antithesis of that system. You cannot graft figs on thorns, nor grapes on thistles.

The greatest of all the lessons to be learned from the United States and the self-governing Dominions is that India must build up her own constitution from her own experience. But before this can happen India must be given a chance of earning her experience. She must also be given electorates capable of reading that experience, and organs through which they can express their views. At present the people of British India have no experience of anything but of the vast unwieldy satrapies in which their races and religions are jumbled together. Before they can really judge of their own future needs, they must be given some experience of self-governing units of a size and character such as have been found necessary wherever responsible government has been achieved on federal lines. When this has been done, India will be in a position to choose for herself, as the result of her own experience, what areas are needed for the achievement of her ideal.

Let me illustrate my meaning from the case of the United Provinces, in the plan proposed in the Joint Address. Four self-governing States are to be created within that Province: Oudh, Benares, the Doab, and Meerut, with an average population of about 11,000,000 each. To each of these Governments, is to be given certain specific functions, revenues and powers of taxation. The old Province and the existing Government are to remain in being, administering all the functions which have not been transferred. But at stated intervals those reserved functions and correlative revenues are to be transferred to the self-governing States, as their Governments demonstrate their capacity for the additional burden.

The last powers to be transferred are Justice and Police. When the States are ready to assume these, the time will have come when Indian statesmen from all the States, and also from the Principalities, must come together to frame a constitution under which the Government of India itself can be made responsible to an Indian Electorate. India will then know who her real leaders are. She will also have developed a real public opinion based on experience. Above all, she will have electorates, legislatures and ministries through whom that public opinion can find expression. The time will have gone when any handful of people can claim to express the voice of India.

Thus when the accredited statesmen of India assemble in Convention to frame the National Constitution, they will have seen the working of self-governing States of the kind which have been found necessary in other federal unions. But the old satrapies will still be in existence; and India can make her choice in the full light of experience. And three possible courses will then be open from which to choose. One will be to abolish the smaller states and merge them again in the old Province. Or else India can decide to keep the States and let the Old Provinces go. There is however a third and quite possible course upon which her assembled statesmen may decide, which has been suggested to me, since the Joint Address was drafted, by an eminent historian and political thinker.

The Indian Community is so much vaster than any which has yet achieved federal self-government, that experience may well prove that between the Central Government and the District, not one but two areas and organs of provincial self-government may be needed. It will be quite open for the convention which drafts the final constitution to decide that Indian society needs the Province on the scale of present satrapies *between the Central Government and the self-governing State.* An Indian nation constituted on these lines would then have a federal government responsible to an Indian electorate, and provincial governments for communities of forty or fifty millions responsible to provincial electorates, and State governments for communities of about 10,000,000 responsible to state electorates.

As to the needs and merits of so novel an arrangement it is fruitless to speculate. The only criterion is experience. But that experience will not be available, unless, in the period of transition, India is allowed to test the value of self-governing States similar to those of the U.S.A. and of the Dominions, in which some unity of race and language and even religion is possible. The governing principle of all arrangements now made should be to enable the people of India, when the time comes for the final step, to shape her own constitution for herself from beginning to end, in the light not of abstract speculations, nor of random quotations from political writers, but of knowledge of her own needs and conditions hardly earned in the field of experience. The priceless gift which statesmanship can give her at this juncture, is a scheme of government in which that experience can be earned, and institutions through which its lessons can be read and expressed.

The proposals set forth in the Joint Address were framed not only to provide a common ground upon which Europeans and Indians could join hands irrespective of race, but also to promote discussion. It is, however, useless to promote discussion between people who are not from the outset prepared to recast their ideas. There are, as I have said elsewhere, things which I should like to have seen added, and others which I should prefer to have seen excluded, in the twelve points to which the signatories subscribed. Having now read and heard volumes of discussion on these proposals, there is, so far, one point only upon which, at the moment of writing, I should wish to modify the original draft submitted to the signatories. I refer to the last part of article three in which it is said that the 'areas *must* be settled at the moment 'when the first instalment of responsible government is 'granted.' Of the soundness of the views given in the last few pages I have since been convinced by the gentleman to whom I have referred. Had his views been before me at the time, I should not have advised the signatories to adopt these words. It is, I conceive, a duty to those who asked my advice, to tell not only them but the public of any point upon which I have since been brought to think that my advice was wrong.

IX

ADMINISTRATIVE MECHANISM AND ITS RECONSTRUCTION.

We have now reached a point at which it will be convenient to notice one formidable criticism which cuts at the root of the whole principle upon which these suggestions are based. It is from the pen of an experienced administrator whose remarks on the subject are as follows:—

> Finally, my experience as an administrator condemns the scheme, as alien to the present structure of the administration. Due to historical reasons which it is unnecessary to specify, the functions of government are interwoven in a complete fabric and are not separate garments capable of division. There are no vertical lines along which the fabric can be divided. The district staff are the main threads running throughout the whole.
>
> No official can satisfactorily serve two masters whose instructions will be conflicting, without neglecting the interests of one. There might be some possibility of success with two entirely separate staffs each responsible to its own government, which is surely the case in the parallels mentioned by you, but none for a single staff responsible to two governments, which must be the case until Indian sentiment changes and until India can afford the more expensive duplicate establishments. Without the active support of the district officer, the progress of the departments of agriculture and co-operative credit would be seriously handicapped. How is it possible to divorce the management of forests, so intimately connected with the well-being of the people, from the general administration?

The argument, as I understand it, is as follows. The various functions of government are parts of a garment woven without seam which cannot be separated from each other. The Public Works Department, the Irrigation Department, the Forest Department, the Agricultural Department, the Educational

Department, etc., must all be kept in relation by the general control of the Revenue Department, *i.e.* the Commissioners and Collectors and Board of Revenue. Separation of any one department from the rest is alien to the present structure of the Administration.

This reasoning admirably illustrates the point I have made on a previous page, that the Government of a Dependency with its mainspring in England, develops administrative mechanism of a type suited to itself. A responsible Government which takes its impetus from an electorate of its own requires a mechanism of a different type. For responsible government involves a system under which one minister controls irrigation, another forests, a third agriculture, and a fourth education. Harmony between these departments must be secured by the joint authority of the Cabinet under the leadership of the Premier. It cannot be secured by the district officers, who must eventually come under one minister, whose sudordinates cannot control the officers ranked under his colleagues.

I suggest that these difficulties can be overcome by the expedient suggested in the Joint Address. In the last chapter it was urged that existing provincial areas are the natural product of the system under which India has been governed as a Dependency of England. The administrative mechanism is also a product of that system. The solution will be found, in taking provincial areas or States suitable for popular government, in giving them electorates with legislatures and executives responsible thereto, and in leaving those executives to develop departments and administrative mechanism suitable to the needs of responsible government.

In any case the argument is least applicable to the first instalment of functions, because those have already been delegated in some measure to the district boards. So far as the reserved functions are concerned, which remain in the hands of the old Government, it will have leisure in which to rearrange its organization with a view to a more complete separation of one function from another, in order to facilitate their successive transfer to the State ministries. The process will consist in gradually divesting the district officers of functions and of appropriating them to specific departments. In the end, the district officer would be left with his general responsibility for maintaining order, and would only pass at the last stage to the control of the State ministry.

This criticism admits that the separation of these functions from each other is largely a question of expense. I agree. The whole system, as at present established, is dominated by the motive of keeping within the limits of an unelastic revenue. And the reason why the revenue is unelastic is twofold. In the first place the taxing authority is unrepresentative. An alien and unrepresentative Government must keep down its expenses to the lowest possible point It has abandoned large sources of revenue which can be tapped by elective authorities. But intense economy, especially in capital expenditure, has also dwarfed the growth of revenues. The institution of authorities, able to raise and spend more because they are elective, will lead to an expansion of existing resources as in Japan. But in any case, without incurring additional expense, there can be no real change in the direction of popular government. Unless the policy proclaimed by the Secretary of State is to be renounced, additional expense must be faced. The resources of the country will bear it, and will expand in response to a more generous public expenditure. Poverty need arrest political progress in India no more than it has done in Japan These conclusions are based upon a study of the revenue system which I have made elsewhere.*

If a real instalment of responsible government is to be given, it must carry with it powers of imposing new taxation. Self-government implies self-taxation. No power of voting will create a sense of responsibility in electorates, unless it involves power to order an

* Studies of Indian Government, No. 3.

increase of service to be rendered, coupled with a power conferred on the elective authority to impose the additional cost on the class from which the voters are drawn. There are two ways in which this may be done. Certain taxes capable of expansion, and roughly commensurate in their present yield to the cost of the duties transferred, may be handed over. The other and simpler plan is to hand over a proportion of the existing consolidated revenue commensurate to the powers transferred. This lump sum would grow with the general growth of revenue. If the Provincial State Government desired to spend more on a service, *e.g.* primary education, than the growth of this revenue justified, then it must have certain sources of new taxation upon which to draw. The excise and power to increase cesses on land are the obvious sources. The essential point is that the new sources of revenue to be drawn upon should involve imposts which the voters themselves will feel.

In order to build up and develop electorates in India the governments responsible thereto must have powers of taxation of their own. But the ministries must also have officers of their own, drawn, of course, from the existing services, but reorganized in departments of a type suitable for control by cabinets responsible to legislatures and electorates. I scarcely see how else the change necessary in the structure of the existing mechanism can be managed. Nor do I see how ministers, legislators, and electors are to develop a real sense of responsibility for the functions entrusted to them, unless they have officers of their own distinct from those of the old governments. The arrangement whereby the District Boards have discharged their functions through the existing departments of government, has I believe gone far to destroy their value, as a factor in educating members and electors to a sense of responsibility.

THE TRAINING-GROUND OF ELECTORATES.

The first step, then, is to call into existence Governments responsible to electorates in each of the States, and transfer to them certain functions and revenues. The crux of the problem is to create electorates competent to bear the whole burden of government in India. A failure to realize the full significance of this truth has operated, I believe, to delay the progress of India towards self-government. How often, for instance, does one hear it said that the transfer to Indians of more responsible offices is an important step in that direction! Now let me say at once that I am in favour of reducing the number of British officials in India to the lowest point compatible with the maintenance of British authority, so long as, and in so far as, the Indian Administration is responsible to the British Parliament. I should like to see this done, if for no other reason, because England can ill spare this continuous drain on her best administrative talent. But Indian officials might be appointed to every office under the Viceroy, without advancing India one step on the road to responsible government. It is not in the Civil Service that the future rulers of India are going to be trained. Personally, I have yet to be convinced that India is going to find its leaders in the ranks of retired officials. It is not men trained in the Russian bureaucracy who are going to lead Russians from anarchy to orderly government. Those who are urging the appointment of more Indians to Commissionerships, Collectorships, and other posts of responsibility, *as a step preliminary to self-government, and as one which must be taken in advance of all others*, are, in my opinion, simply off the track. Responsible government is possible in so far as there are electorates adequate to the burden. Given such electorates, men capable of leadership will not be wanting, though they will not be found in the ranks of officials. If your bureaucracy were at once Indian throughout and also the most highly trained in the world, you would not be in sight of responsible government until you had evolved responsible electorates. The key to the problem before us is electoral reform. Civil Service reform is another question altogether.

In a previous chapter I urged that electorates cannot be developed merely by the kind of education given in schools and colleges. It is only by exercise of some responsibility that electorates can be rendered fit to exercise more. Such responsibility may and indeed must be limited, to begin with; but in order to have any effect it must be real. Representative government hinges on the fact that electorates cannot do things for themselves. They must have representatives through whom to do them. Those representatives they must be able to dismiss by their votes, for otherwise their agents would not be responsible to the voters. But political responsibility is always a two-sided relation. If it means that executives and legislatures are responsible to the electorates for carrying out their mandates, it means no less that the electorates are responsible to their representatives for rendering them the necessary obedience and providing them with the funds and powers. A genuine responsibility is always bilateral. It is not enough for an electorate to instruct its representatives to build more roads, to multiply schools and colleges, or to settle contentious issues this way or that. They must also learn by experience that these things cannot be done unless they are prepared to see those representatives impose taxation upon them, and to acquiesce in the exercise of powers without which their elected rulers cannot give effect to their mandates. Just as the electorate must from time to time have the power of dismissing its agents, so must the agents themselves be able to retire and refuse to serve unless the electorate will grant them the means and powers required to give effect to its mandate. The system must be so simple as to bring home this elementary position as quickly as possible to the electorates.

In various quarters it is strongly argued that electorates must first be prepared by experience in the field of local government. The advocates of this view would begin, where Lord Ripon tried to begin thirty years ago, by making district, village and town boards really responsible to electorates. And their reason for this position is partly because, like my friend whose letter I quoted in the last chapter, they cannot picture a transitional system, under which some provincial functions are transferred to electoral authorities while others are reserved to the existing Provincial Governments.

In order to examine these positions it is necessary to realize that the spheres of local and political government are divided by a line that is fairly clear. The field which can be covered by local government is much the same in all countries. It is of necessity confined to the settlement of administrative details, and the framing of minor regulations and bye-laws inseparable therefrom. The London County Council is perhaps the largest and most important body of the kind in the world. Its population and revenues exceed those of many sovereign States. On education alone its annual expenditure is in millions of pounds: and yet if it were empowered to pass an Education Act, or to change the constitution of the minor municipalities within its area, its whole status and character would be radically changed. It would then have assumed functions now vested in Parliament and discharged through the Minister of Education, and the President of the Local Government Board. It would have outstepped the limits of Local Government, properly so called, and have entered the field of a Provincial Government;—a thing which would be quite possible, if the United Kingdom were parcelled out at the same time into a number of similar provinces containing five million people and upwards.

A Provincial Government is an organ which deals with political subjects, that is to say, with questions of principle, upon which not merely the interests but also the consciences of great sections of the community are at issue. There is all the difference between a body which administers roads, sanitation and schools, and one which can decide, by the measures it passes, the relative positions of Hindus and Mahomedans on Municipal Bodies, the principles upon which religion is to be handled, or the extent to which a particular language is to be used in schools. You could not hand over the functions of the Local Government Board and the Board of Education to the County Councils of Wales, nor empower them to pass Education Acts and Local Government Acts. They would be too small, and the diversity created would be too great. But all these powers might well be given to a Provincial Government representing the whole of Wales. Such a body would then be exercising political powers. It would stand above the field of Local Government, and of mere administrative detail, such as can be delegated to a County Council or District Board. Thus there is a clear line between the administrative functions which can be delegated to a local body, even so large and important as the London County Council, and the political functions which can be exercised by Provinces, which may be as small as Prince Edward Island in Canada, or Rhode Island in the United States.

The same is equally true of India. The creation of local authorities and the definition of their constitutions and powers is a political function. It is none the less one which cannot be undertaken by the Government of India, but must be relegated to Provincial Governments. In recent years the educational policy of the Government of the United Provinces and municipal legislation have involved the settlement of sharp issues between the Hindu and Moslem Communities. In such legislation the Provincial Government decides the nature of the minor revenues assigned to these bodies, and within what limits such revenues can be increased or reduced. It has also to decide what grants from Government revenues are to be placed at the disposal of the Boards, and especially the principle upon which such grants are to be apportioned amongst the numerous local authorities. The decision of such issues cannot be left to the district and municipal boards. To them is entrusted the construction and maintenance of roads and drainage systems, the control of building, etc., and the making of bye-laws dealing with these subjects. In the educational sphere, it is left to the Boards to decide where to open new schools, where to close schools, where to aid them, how to staff them, how to train the staff, where to build new buildings, how to build them, and so on. In many of these matters they are required to satisfy certain minima conditions laid down by the Local Self-government Board or the Educational Department.

It will perhaps help to elucidate the matter, if we take one example showing the kind of question which cannot be relegated to local authorities, but must, because it is political, be decided by a Provincial Government.

Before the Muhammadan invasions from the north the principal language of these provinces was Hindi, a language closely allied to the ancient Sanscrit, closely associated therefore with Hinduism, and written in the Nagari script. For the purpose of administration the Muhammadans took many words of Hindi and compounded them with many Persian and Arabic words of their own. The result was Hindustani, the language of administration, of the camp and of matters of everyday life; and this language was written both in the Persian and also in the Nagari script. The result was a *lingua franca* which, though written by Hindus in the Nagari, and by Muhammadans in the Persian character, is in conversation available to both for the limited purposes of ordinary life. For literary expression, or for the purpose of rational discussion, whether of politics, religion or morals, the Hindu resorts to Hindi words, while the Muhammadan on the other hand uses Urdu words of Persian and Arabic origin. Thus it is only for the most ordinary purposes that Hindus and Muhammadans converse in a common language. For all higher purposes the one converses in Hindi, and the other in Urdu; and each is written in a different script.

These conditions occasion no serious problem in the earlier stages of a child's education. So long as teaching is confined to simple words and ideas the common basis of Hindustani provides all that is needed. The text-books can be printed in both the Nagari and Persian scripts, the children of Hindus and Muhammadans can thus learn to read either or both. But when the child begins to pass beyond the stage of simple words and ideas, the restricted vocabulary and the simplified grammar of Hindustani begin to break down, and his teaching must be given, and his text-books must be worded, more and more either in Hindi or else in Urdu. The choice raises the whole issue between the two religions. A similar position might easily have arisen in the south-east of Europe, where members of the Latin and Greek Churches mix. Such a population might have evolved a mixed patois of Greek and Latin words for the purpose of ordinary conversation. But the moment that education had reached a certain point, parents of the Roman religion would wish to have their children taught in the language of Latin origin, in which the liturgies of their Church were expressed, while those of the Greek Church would wish their children to be instructed in the Greek tongue.

In either religion are extremists, who would, if they could, secure a decision in favour of the language of their own religion, and the suppression of the other language as a medium of education. No reasonable person is likely to listen to such views; and, therefore, the practical question arises, whether the bifurcation into Hindi by Hindu children, and into Urdu by Muhammadan children, is to take place before the stage of vernacular education, as provided by Government, is passed, and, if so, at what point. In 1876 and again in 1903 the Government of the U.P. tried to solve the problem by insisting on the policy of prescribing readers in the limited common language. A committee was appointed in 1910 to draw up a scheme for the preparation of new readers, and a majority of the members "held that in higher readers some simple "passages of literary merit should be interspersed with "lessons written in the common language, and that "such passages must of necessity be in distinctive "Urdu or Hindi." *

The Government, however, adhered to its previous position, and dissolved the committee. In the next four years the whole position was explored by several committees, and became the subject of wide discussion. From these discussions emerged a distinct preponderance of opinion in favour of bifurcation before the child had passed the stage of class IV. But as to the exact point at which the bifurcation should begin, and as to the way in which the text-books should be prepared, a variety of different schemes were produced. Obviously the question was one which admitted of settlement in a great variety of different ways, each of which might be regarded as more or less favourable to either of the rival religions.

With all this mass of varied opinions before him, the Lieutenant-Governor sat down in 1914 to decide the question. He began by stating the principles upon which he proposed to base his decision as follows:—

> The conclusions of the Lieutenant-Governor then are that—
>
> (*a*) The common or Hindustani language, printed in either Persian or Nagari type, should be used in the primary readers, so long as it has anything to teach;
>
> (*b*) When the common language has nothing more to teach, the pupil should learn to read Urdu or Hindi according to the wish of his parents;
>
> (*c*) The readers printed in the common language and used up to the end of class IV do not allow the pupil to leave his primary school with that mental equipment which it is desired to give him.
>
> In other words, while His Honour accepts the policy of teaching the common language so long as possible, he

* Report of the D.P.I. for the year ending 31st March, 1916, p. 2.

believes that bifurcation may be deferred too long. At present, in his opinion, it is unduly deferred, and valuable time is lost reading and re-reading a primer when it has ceased to serve any purpose as a means of progressive education. He considers therefore that bifurcation should begin a little earlier than is now the case. Primers on the lines of those now in use, printed in either character, should be retained for classes I and II; and there is also required for use above those classes, what for brevity may be designated a senior reader in the common language, similarly printed, and graduated in difficulty, so far as possible, from the beginning onwards. All these books should contain lessons in prose only. When the teacher is satisfied that a class has mastered the senior reader, he should at once promote them to one of two supplementary readers. Such promotion would not ordinarily come until the end of class III, and may even be later, according to the capacity of the pupils. The sole test should be whether the class has mastered all that it can learn from the senior reader; and it is for the master, and the master alone, to say when this happens; but it should usually be possible for the last half of the year in class IV to be spent on the supplementary readers. These should be composed in distinctive Urdu and Hindi respectively. They should contain both prose and verse, taken as far as possible from standard authors; but religious and didactic passages should be avoided, so as to respect the sensibilities of Hindus who may be taking Urdu, or Muhammadans who may be reading the Hindi course The preparation of the supplementary readers should be undertaken as soon as possible, by the Provincial Text-Book Committee, who will have the advantage of studying the readers which were drafted by the committee presided over by Pandit Rama Shankar.

The course of study thus indicated will, Sir James Meston trusts, maintain the principle of elementary teaching in a simple common language so long as such teaching has an educative value; while it will ensure that the pupil leaves class IV with an education which will not only be of practical value to him in after-life, but will also open for him the door to the literature of his religion and his ancestors. This was, he feels sure, the aim of all the members of Mr. Justice Pigott's Committee, though the attempt at reconciling divergent views led to a form

> of compromise which would have presented difficulties in practice. The alternative he has decided to adopt will, he believes, not prove open to this objection; but he does not pretend to hope that it will please all schools of thought. *The question has reached a point where mutual concessions seem impossible; and it is clearly the duty of the Government to formulate a decision, making the interests of the child its sole consideration, and the progress of sound education its only aim.**

In the joint scheme it is proposed to transfer minimum powers at the outset to ministries responsible to legislatures and electorates for areas such as could serve as the future self-governing Provinces of a United States of India. These minimum powers would include the control of local government, and of primary education. This does not mean that they would be nothing but enlarged district and municipal boards, but the very opposite. It means that these new and popular Governments would be charged with the control of local authorities, which from the nature of the case those bodies cannot exercise for themselves. The State Governments would be bodies charged with the settlement of political questions such as cannot be relegated to district, village and town boards. They could, for instance, pass an Education Act, and in doing so would have to face and settle all the disputes between Hindus and Moslems, which the recent legislation in the United Provinces has roused.

They would also, from time to time, have to face the invidious task of apportioning Government grants between the various local authorities. This apportionment is now determined by settlements made in 1914, which expire in 1919. In that year a State Government in the U.P. would have to decide how much of its own revenues could be spared for grants-in-aid to the boards, and (a far more formidable task) how that sum is to be divided amongst all the bodies in question. The settlement of 1914 was an example of administrative skill carried to its highest point. It

* Lieutenant-Governor's Resolution of August 25th, 1914, p. 25.

was a masterpiece of applied statistical science, based upon an infinity of data and patiently worked out to the last detail. It is almost too perfect for the rougher conditions of popular government, which means government by laymen. Without a long official training it would be difficult for a minister to master the technical calculations; and it is safe to add that in no popular assembly in the world would more than a handful of members be found able to grasp the explanations, assuming that the minister was competent to give them. Even in the British Parliament, which, in point of education and intelligence, is inferior to no other elective Chamber, a minister would be most likely forced to adopt some cruder and therefore less equitable basis of division, such, for instance, as population. He would shrink from the dangers of asking members to ratify a scheme which few or none of them would understand. As a piece of distributive justice, the settlement made would most likely compare unfavourably with that which was made by the science, exactitude and industry of the I.C.S.

Another feature of this settlement to be noticed is the position of those who made it. They were men disposed by nature and training to justice; but had they been otherwise they had no temptation to injustice. Their tenure of office was not affected by the manner in which their division of the grant was received, and by that division they had nothing remotely to gain or lose. The consent of the legislature was not even required, for the calculations were examined and finally ratified by the Lieutenant-Governor in the quiet detachment of his own study.

A glance at countries where provincial self-government exists, will reveal the totally different position of a minister holding office by virtue of a majority of legislators who are looking to their constituents for re-election. Not merely his own tenure of office, but that of his colleagues, would be affected by that issue and might even depend on it. The minister would not be called upon to satisfy the whole body of members, but rather the majority who keep him in office. The fate of a ministry often depends upon a margin of votes from certain particular districts, and the voters of those districts may convince their members that their re-election will depend upon how far they secure from the Government a generous share of the plunder. And thus begins the sordid struggle which Americans aptly call the fight for the pork barrel. This struggle appears but little in debate. It proceeds behind the closed doors of ministers and whips, who are given to understand, by no uncertain signs, that the continued support of this or that member will depend on the share of the plunder given to his constituents. Such divisions of public money test the capacity of a people for doing justice between themselves. But it also develops that capacity by exercise, assuming that the test is not so severe as to break it down altogether. A complete and final collapse of justice leads to disorder.

The third and most instructive example is afforded by the controversy between the protagonists of Hindi or Urdu. It is issues like these which test and exercise the faculty of self-government to the full. For mere money is capable of division, even if the division be unjust. But in life there are issues, moral, religious and political, deep as the well-springs of human belief, such as are not capable of division. There are principles upon which those who hold them will be willing to accept an adverse ruling from a third party who stands outside the controversy, because, knowing his detachment, they believe in his justice. It may well happen, however, that they would go to extremes rather than accept that same ruling at the hands of the party to which they are opposed.

The relative positions of Hindi and Urdu in the vernacular schools, which the Lieutenant-Governor of the United Provinces had to decide in 1914, may be taken as a typical example of such issues. No pains were spared to elicit from educated Indians, whether by means of committees or discussions in the Legislative Councils, an expression of all their different opinions. The Lieutenant-Governor studiously exposed himself to the influence of these various views. He saturated his mind in all the reports and speeches stating the reasons upon which they were based. And then having done so he wrote: "Mutual concessions "seem impossible; *and it is 'clearly the duty of the Govern-" "ment to formulate a decision.'*" And so he recorded a decision which was not exactly any of those which lay before him, but one, the terms of which he had framed for himself. And because he was a foreigner, a member of neither religion, unbiased, therefore, in his interests, absolutely detached in his point of view, and universally recognized to be so, his decision was accepted almost without demur and certainly without resistance on the part of either of the religions involved. In this manner the question was decided for the time being, though in future years it is sure to be raised again in some form or other.

There are certain features of the case which from the standpoint of this enquiry call for remark. If a question at issue can be settled by willing agreement of *all* the parties concerned, that is usually the best possible decision. But the fact that such settlements are not always possible is too often ignored. The existence of law courts backed by the sheriff, policeman and soldier is a standing witness to the fact. And as may be seen in the present case, there are issues beyond the jurisdiction of courts, which cannot be settled by agreement, but which cannot be left unsettled without inflicting grievous injury on third parties and on future generations. Such issues a Government must sooner or later decide on lines not wholly acceptable to one party or even perhaps to either. This was what Washington meant when he said, 'Influence is not government.' The influence of rulers should be used to the full to induce an agreement between the parties at issue. But failing such agreement the time comes when Government must decide, or civilisation will stagnate or decay. And the decision must be accepted by a body of opinion strong enough to neutralise resistance, not necessarily because the decision is approved, but rather because the majority of thinking men are resolved to uphold the authority of Government.

The decision in question was not the one suggested by any of the parties concerned. And yet it was accepted by all those parties because it was made by a man in whose anxiety to mete out impartial justice everyone believed. But it was not merely in this justice of one individual they trusted. That individual was responsible to the Governor-General, the Secretary of State, the British Parliament, and finally to public opinion in England. The first could advise his dismissal, the second could dismiss him, the third could exact it, the fourth could demand it. The acceptance of such decisions in India is not based merely on confidence in the justice of an individual officer. It is based to an even greater extent on confidence that an authority six thousand miles away will appoint officers who are just, and remove those who fail in their charge. The manner in which decisions of such issues are accepted in India, is largely due to the fact that those who make them are answerable to an authority remote from the seat of controversy. Let anyone consider whether this decision could have been so made and so accepted if the same individual had been a prime minister, responsible not to the British Government, but to an electorate in the United Provinces, and dependent for the tenure of his office on the support of a majority in the Legislative Council, elected by a majority of the voters. Imagine the position of the same individual, with the same character and reputation in this wholly different position, and one then begins to see how much depends upon the fact that he is now responsible to an authority which is detached and impartial because it is foreign.

It is this that is meant by saying that the Government of India is in trust. The acceptance of decisions made by that Government between two rival sections in India is due to the confidence in the trustees, by reason of their disinterest in and detachment from the issues at stake. Where questions are at issue between

India and the British trustee, as in the case of the cotton duties, this confidence is wanting.

The immediate administration of vernacular schools, within limits carefully prescribed, has been entrusted to District and Municipal Boards. Within those limits, they are charged with the task of making decisions which must often affect minor matters at issue between Hindus and Moslems. They might support Maktabs at the expense of Pathsalas. A religious majority on a Board might abuse its position in appointing the teachers. But the crucial decisions on matters of policy, such as that dealt with in the present case, are made for them by an authority responsible to a Government and public opinion outside India.

In the Joint Address a method has been suggested whereby decisions of this class might be relegated to a ministry responsible to a provincial electorate, and removable from office by the vote of a majority of legislators elected by a majority of voters. For the purpose of this enquiry it is useful to consider how the decision in question would have to be made under these circumstances. It is fair to assume that the same pains would be taken to elicit opinion as was taken in the case of the present Government. An Indian Minister of Education, either a Muhammadan or a Hindu, would then draft the terms of a decision, which would be discussed, and probably modified, in the Cabinet Council. The Government supporters would be sounded as to whether they would be prepared to back the decision. And, if the Government were wise, means would also be taken to ascertain how far the minority in opposition and their constituents would be prepared to accept it. And all this time, it must be remembered the point at issue would be the subject of a burning public controversy. Meetings would be held, angry speeches would be made, and bitter articles would be written. Ministers would scarcely think of finding the best solution. Rather their efforts would be directed to finding one which their supporters would be prepared to back, but such as would not drive the minority of voters into an active or passive resistance of the law when passed. For the decision would have to take the form of a Bill to be debated by the legislature in open session; and upon the acceptance or rejection of the Bill the fate of the ministry would depend. The existence of the ministry itself would certainly hang on the issue. The best decision would scarcely be reached in the heat of the controversy. The best result attainable in practice would be the acceptance of some decision by the minority when they had been voted down. And that acceptance would depend, partly on their patriotism, upon their desire to support a system under which Indians could settle Indian questions for themselves, but largely also on the tolerance of the majority, on their willingness not to abuse their power shown by making concessions which would render the decision tolerable to the minds and consciences of their opponents.

When compared with the smooth, detached and accurate working of a good bureaucracy, responsible government is an ugly business, even in the British Isles. Why then, if you have such a system in India, should you seek to replace it by responsible government? An answer to that question can only be found by reference to the ultimate aims which government should seek.

Some light may be thrown on the subject by considering an imaginary case in another field. As anyone knows who has been in an army when rations are short and soldiers grow hungry, the question of apportioning the food available has a wonderful effect in revealing the character of different men and different units. In exceptional regiments you will find the men stinting themselves, so as to be sure that comrades, perhaps weaker than themselves, have enough. In such regiments the officers will readily leave the apportionment of the rations to the men themselves.

And now let us turn to a regiment of average men, some better and some worse. In many regiments, unhappily, there is pilfering in the cook-house when rations are short. In such a regiment, if the division of rations be left to the men themselves, some selfishness will be shewn. The weaker and more unselfish will not get all they should. The justice done is rough and imperfect. There is some bickering which is rather squalid, but no positive violence, no actual starvation of the weaker men. So the officers leave the men to work out the division for themselves, trusting that, given sufficient time, they will learn to do the thing more fairly. And experience, indeed, teaches that, given time, this will be the result. This regiment, if the officers do not interfere, will gradually approximate to the standard of the first regiment described.

Thirdly, we may take the other extreme and exceptional case, that of a regiment where the men in the cook-house eat their fill, and when the remainder does reach the rest, the stronger take so much that the weaker or less selfish actually starve and go sick. Or else there are constant disputes that end in a fight. In the case of such a regiment the officers must watch the food in the cook-house, to see that it is not pilfered by the cooks. And when the food is prepared, they must measure out the proportion justly due to each of the men, and watch while they eat it, to see that it is not taken from them. Externally, justice and order will prevail. The scene presented in the cook-house, and by the men at their meals, will contrast favourably with that presented in the second regiment described. There will be no unfairness, no ugly bickering, no squalid disputes, no pilfering by the cooks, and generally less waste. And yet results so secured by supervision of officers, however necessary, are almost barren of hope for the future. True they will enable the men to see what justice and order mean; but when that is done, the spirit of fairness will develop but little, until they are able to assume some responsibility for dividing the food themselves. To become more just they must have opportunities of injustice; and unless they can be given some such responsibility, and some such opportunity, they will never begin to realize what a hateful thing injustice is.

In this fanciful picture is implicit the philosophy of freedom, the whole issue at stake in the present war. If material development, visible order, mechanical efficiency and financial economy in the present and in the immediate future are the ends in view, then the Prussians are right. The decisions of Government should be left to a handful of men of the clearest intellect and the strongest character. And, as in Prussia, the Government from first to last must aim by all means in its power to foster a habit of unquestioning submission in the people they rule.

If, on the other hand, the character of the people at large, the development in common men of their innate sense of justice, and of their faculty of doing justice to each other at their own expense, is the end in view, then Government will decide nothing which it can relegate to the decision of those people themselves, without permitting a break-down of social order. The choice lies between results we can handle and see, reduce to cash values, depict in reports and tabulate in figures, and those which cannot be seen, measured or described, or ever be perceived in the span of our own lives. You can measure railways in miles, and their earnings in cash. You can enumerate the acres brought under irrigation, estimate lives saved from famine and disease, and exhibit an unprecedented growth in the population. You can dwell on the increase of schools and scholars, the improvement in tillage and in crops per acre, and the growth of industrial undertakings. There is something so definite and tangible in it all; and rulers who compile such reports have the satisfaction of knowing that they are telling of things which they themselves have helped to achieve. The effect which a system has on the character of a people can never be stated in figures, and can scarcely be perceived in the life of a single administrator. It is in the end a question between ponderable and imponderable values, between things to be seen with the eye, and those to be seen only in dreams, between seed that the sower may reap, and that which shall only whiten to harvest long after he is dust and his memory forgotten amongst men. The heaven-sent ruler is one with an ear deaf to audible praise, an eye fixed upon a goal which he shall not reach, and above all, an indomitable faith in the power for growth in the weakest of his kind.

The issue is between immediate efficiency, a rapid, material and calculable progress, and the slow incalculable growth of character. But in the long run there is no conflict between the policy which looks to develop the character of people, and that which seeks to promote their efficiency. The policy which looks only to efficiency and measurable progress, ends by destroying the objects it pursues. If Englishmen have established order in countries which could not create it for themselves, it is only by virtue of qualities developed through ages, in which their own characters have been tempered and moulded by their own mistakes. Such justice as Englishmen have imported to India has been learned in the doing of much injustice among themselves. And if Englishmen know how to get things done, that lesson has slowly been learned by enduring the results of their own neglect. It is much to have stopped bloodshed in India, to have created order to have enforced justice, to have given her a modern equipment and to have set her on the path of material progress. But the character of a people will not always stand still, even in the East. If it does not get better it will surely get worse. England cannot always provide these benefits for India without fatally enfeebling the character of her people. Neither material equipment nor even the enforcement of peace and justice between man and man, are ends in themselves. They are hardly means. They are rather the beginnings of means. The end is simply the character of the people, which is formed in the process of adjusting their relations to each other. The establishment of social order from without renders it vastly easier for a beginning to be made. Suddenly to impose upon strength and faculties still unexercised the whole burden of maintaining order, is to jeopardise the conditions under which responsible government can begin. But unless or until genuine responsibilities are imposed on those few who are in some sort able to assume them, neither the capacity for making decisions will develop, nor yet the numbers of those who show promise of developing such capacity. All minor ends must be subordinated to that of fostering this native capacity, which, as it grows, will in ages to come yield a harvest of native efficiency and capacity for justice. Without travail there is no birth, and the glories of motherhood are hard to discern in the throes of delivery. 'Seek ye first the Kingdom of God and all things else shall be added unto you' is a saying as true in politics as in any other department of life. One final truth issues from the commonplace details set down in these pages. If effect on the growth of character is to be taken as the criterion of policy, it is not enough for Government to consult the people. The burden of making decisions must be imposed upon those in some sort able to decide.

Even amongst the wisest and most experienced of those who have dedicated their lives to India there is much shadowy thinking on this subject. Some months ago publicity was given to the following remarks by the present writer:—

"The policy of the British Government is to "develop (nationalist) opinion and to allow it to "influence policy more and more. The responsibility "of final decision it still reserves to itself. But it "now looks to a time, however remote, when it will "be able to transfer that responsibility to a section of "Indians sufficiently large, disinterested, and capable "of sound political judgment to assume it."

These words seem to have occasioned no little alarm in the mind of so old and sincere a friend of Indian aspirations as Sir Courtenay Ilbert. In the Imperial supplement to *The Manchester Guardian*, issued on March 20, 1917, Sir Courtenay Ilbert wrote the following comments on these words:—

> What does the writer exactly mean when he says that self-government is the aim to which British policy in India must be directed? . . . It is a pity that he did not make his meaning more clear, because his words

> may be quoted against him, and because self-government in the colonial sense would be a false ideal to pursue. India cannot copy patterns supplied by Canada, Australia, and South Africa. India must be developed on Indian lines, upon lines appropriate to Indian conditions, lines very different from those on which the great democracies in the self-governing dominions are running their course. In marking out those lines regard must always be had to Indian political opinion, which, as Mr. Curtis justly observes, is a reality, and an important reality, difficult though it may be to ascertain, and unsatisfactory as may be some of its features. It is a curious and puzzling blend, produced by the interfusion and interaction of Western and Eastern thought, abounding in paradoxes and contradictions.

This veteran exponent of liberalism cannot bring himself to regard *self-government in the colonial sense* as other than a false ideal for India to pursue. In the kindness of his heart he seeks to acquit me of a meaning so dangerous and absurd. Yet that is the only meaning my words will bear, and I must avail myself of this opportunity to repeat that that was the only meaning they were meant to convey.

No sane man wants India to copy *word for word* patterns supplied by Canada, Australia and South Africa. Not so did Australia copy the Canadian Constitution, nor South Africa those of Canada and Australia. They each examined their own conditions, and framed an instrument more or less suited thereto. They worked as engineers must severally work, whether they are designing an internal combustion engine to drive a motor-car, aeroplane, ship or pump. But all were applying one principle, that first reduced to practical form in the British constitution, the principle which seeks to impose responsibility for political decisions on all the members of the community affected by those decisions who are in some sort capable of making them. They are all, in short, expressions of the principle of responsible government. I must say once for all, without any kind of qualification, that the application of that principle as rapidly as possible is for me the only intelligible goal of British policy in

India. Together with the question of self-preservation, of foreign policy and defence, it is the greatest of the problems which this Commonwealth has to face. It is the *articulus stantis aut cadentis republicae*,—the cardinal principle by which this Commonwealth will stand or fall.

What is the other ideal which Sir Courtenay Ilbert, Lord Morley, and the large number of public men who use language like this, have in mind? So far as I can discern it is accurately stated in the words he has quoted from my own letter:—

> 'Broadly speaking, Government is at pains to recognise such opinion as there is. It accepts it where it can, often when it thinks that Nationalist opinion is not the best, ignoring it only where it appears so unsound that to accept and act upon it would lead to disaster. The policy of the British Government is to develope that opinion and to allow it to influence policy more and more. The responsibility of final decision it still reserves to itself.'

Here, it may be observed, is an exact description of the policy actually applied in 1914 to the settlement of the issues between the Hindi and Urdu vernaculars. No pains were spared to elicit Indian views on the subject from those capable of formulating and expressing them. Every phase of Indian opinion was before the Lieutenat-Governor. His mind was steeped in them. Had he been thinking of absolute efficiency in education, regardless of the prejudice in favour of either language, he might, perhaps, have decided in favour of one of them. He recognized the existence and reality of the feeling in favour of their own dialect entertained by each of the two religions. And having done so he made his decision, in discharge of the trust imposed upon him for the interests of his Province by the Imperial Government in England.

If this principle of government is the end-all and be-all of British policy in India, there is little which remains to be done in order to complete its final applicat'on. If, on the other hand, the burden of final decision is ever to be transferred to the people of India themselves there is almost everything to be done. But you will not have done it, or begun to do it, merely by substituting Indian for English officials from the Viceroy downwards Under the present system the responsibility for decision would still be made in obedience to the authority outside India, which has the power to dismiss those officials. To make a beginning you must take certain clearly-defined functions of government, including taxation, and impose the duty of making decisions in respect of those functions on men responsible to, and therefore removable by, electorates all over India. To begin with, these electorates can only include the minority, however small, which is capable of judgment. In respect of the functions imposed upon them, those small electorates must act as the trustees of the majority of their fellow-countrymen, who are as yet incapable of political judgment. No educational means must be neglected to awaken the political consciousness of the classes outside the electorate, and to include them within it as rapidly as they are qualified. But of all those means the most potent will prove to be the spiritual commotion engendered by the system itself. It is the spirit of freedom, moving in the darkness of chaos, that creates light, calls new worlds into being, and peoples them with life and thought. It is as the four winds which blew in the valley of dry bones, till the breath came into them, and they lived, and stood up on their feet, an exceeding great army.

The growth of genuine electorates embracing all religions and all castes will mark the progress of India up the difficult path of responsible government. So too will the disappearance of religious distinctions in those electorates, and the appearance of members of every caste side by side in the same cabinets and legislatures. And the growth in size and quality of the electorates will in practice determine the pace at which functions of increasing gravity can be transferred from the old Governments to the new. Above all it is essential that in this vast community the progress of the forward parts of India must not be tied down to that of the more backward. It is the example of the more progressive communities in successfully discharging weightier functions, which more than anything will stimulate the backward to fresh efforts. There is nothing so contagious as example. Any system, which presupposes a uniform rate of advance to be imposed on the various Provinces, will load the whole of India with fetters. Each must be enabled to advance at its own pace, not merely for its own sake, but rather because it will stimulate the others. And you must be prepared for retreat where you are proved by experience to have gone too far and too fast. Otherwise the courage to experiment and advance will be wanting. But for this there must be faith in the intention to advance; to create and maintain which faith rests with the Parliament of the whole Commonwealth, and for every member of that Commonwealth in all the seven seas, who is mindful of the principle by which it stands or falls. But mere intention is not enough; there must be clearness of vision and thought. "Indian political opinion," says the writer quoted above, "is a curious and puzzling blend, produced by the "interfusion and interaction of Western and Eastern "thought, abounding in paradoxes and contradic-"tions." But the first responsibility of Englishmen is for their own thinking. Now, if ever, it is for us to see to it that our thoughts are neither anxious nor puzzled, are free from all paradoxes and contradictions, and above all true to ourselves, our traditions and our past. But in this we shall fail unless we first state our own ideas with precision, and then apply them to actual and particular cases. 'Influence is not Government.' And that distinction is as valid in India to-day as it was more than a century ago in the United States. Does Sir Courtenay Ilbert mean that we can continue indefinitely to elaborate the machinery through which opinions in India can be rendered accessible to the Government? Does he really think that it will suffice for Government to render itself more and more amenable to the influence of opinions which are often conflicting? And when all this has been done, is Government in the end, finally and for all time, to reserve the responsibility of decision to itself? Is that task of deciding between conflicting interests never to be imposed on people in India themselves? Is the final control of functions like education never to be entrusted to Indians? Is the power to impose new revenues on themselves for the extension of those functions never to be given them? Are they never to be burdened with the difficult task of distributing those revenues between minor authorities? Are controversies between the various religions always to be settled in the end by the officers responsible to a Government in London? To bring these questions to a fine point, take the controversy over Hindi and Urdu described in these pages, which, in some form or other, is certain to rise again and again. Is a time never to arrive when decisions of that order can be made by men responsible to Indians, removable by Indians, or in plain words by an Indian electorate? And if ever electorates prove themselves capable of making and sustaining such decisions, can the process be stopped till all issues, however great, which affect Indians alone, are settled by men responsidle to Indian electorates alone and removable at their bidding?

Freedom, which in its political aspect is responsible government, is a human and not a Western ideal. True it was first conceived and applied in the West. But the truths of religion were first conceived and applied in the East. It was there men learned to worship their common Father at Jerusalem, Mecca and where the Ganges flows. "But the hour cometh, and "now is, when the true worshippers shall worship the "Father in spirit and in truth: for the Father seeketh "such to worship him." The whole earth is the temple of freedom, and the heavens themselves the dome that covers it. Its spirit moves wherever men are learning to do justice to each other, even at the cost of injustice done. A noise and a shaking there will be, as the bones draw together, but a breath is coming from the four winds. The principle that men are responsible to each other is at work, and wherever it works it will grow with exercise. That principle, and no other, applied in detail to the facts of their own lives; has produced the constitutions of free nations. It has raised great armies willing to die, that in their dust that principle may live. And it is upon that principle, and no other, that a constitution which will bring freedom to India must be framed. The text of that constitution will be that neither of Canada, Australia or South Africa. It will 'be developed on Indian lines, upon lines appropriate to Indian conditions.' But that will only be when it is developed by trial of Indian conditions, by the increasing application of one human, unalterable principle of society to Indian facts, by readiness to recognize, not the failure of a principle which cannot fail, but only of the mechanism by which we seek to apply it. And the pace of progress will be in direct proportion to the extent to which the machinery enables us to distinguish failure from success. If there are to be electorates in India, and those electorates are to increase and rise to a fuller sense of the trust imposed on them, then surely they cannot be made too clearly to see that the trust rests on themselves, and what it is. Surely the officers who administer that trust must know what exactly it is for which they are responsible, and to whom. One Executive cannot obey the orders of a Government in England, and also the behests of an Indian electorate. So long as executives exist in India responsible to an authority in England, those executives must spare no pains to elicit and understand Indian opinion in all its varieties. They must steep their minds with knowledge of what is thought and felt by those whom the decision they frame will affect. But when they decide they must be held responsible for their decisions by one authority and one alone. And all the members of every executive must be held responsible to that authority, the Indian no less than the English members.

But the converse proposition is equally important, and no less true. If there are to be executives in India responsible to Indian electorates, they must know clearly what those responsibilities are. And they must be responsible to those electorates so long as they hold office. They cannot be partly responsible to any authority outside India. And the responsibility, which one executive has to its legislature and electorate, must be shared alike by every member of it until he resigns. There can be and must be public divisions in electorates and legislatures. In executives there can be none. A divided executive is the negation of responsible government.

XI

EXTREMISTS AND HOW THEY MEET.

The proposals suggested in the Joint Address are exposed to a fire of criticism from two extremes. Some of the Nationalists have awaked to the fact that the Congress-League scheme contains no element of responsible government. They begin to realize that the hope of India lies in achieving responsible government, and they are anxious that the Provincial Executives should be made responsible to electorates for all their functions at one stroke. They are, therefore, concerned to prove that two Governments cannot exist side by side in the Provinces, the one responsible to electorates for some functions, the other to the Secretary of State for all the rest. Their attitude on this question is reinforced by a desire to obtain the control of police at once.

The more cautious section of Europeans, on the other hand, are anxious to see the promised reforms confined to the sphere of local government. They also are concerned to demonstrate that a specific devolution of some Provincial functions to Governments responsible to electorates, while others are reserved to the Governments responsible to the Secretary of State, is impossible.

Probably they believe that when local authorities have been made responsible to electorates, there are two stages which still remain, and that then Provincial Executives can be made responsible long before a similar change need be made in the sphere of the Government of India. This view, however obvious it may seem, will not, I believe, bear analysis. Why are functions of government in India, and in other countries of a like magnitude, divided between the Central Government and those of Provinces? The answer is twofold. In the case of functions like education, variety of treatment is required to suit the local conditions of different areas. But there is a second and no less important reason. The maintenance of law and order is the basic function of Government. It is for the performance of that duty, first and foremost, that the Governor-General-in-Council is responsible to Parliament through the Secretary of State. But the organization required for the purpose is so vast that it cannot be managed in all its details from one centre like Delhi or Simla. It must, for administrative reasons, be devolved on Provincial Governments, which are in fact nothing more nor less than local departments of the Government of India. That Government can remain responsible to Parliament, only so long as the Provincial Governments remain responsible to itself for the *final* control of Police.

I lay particular stress on the word *final*, because I am not assuming that the police need always remain as one closely organized department from the Inspector-General to the village chaukidar. I see no reason why the management of the village constables should not be relegated to the new elective authorities from the outset. Then there are the great bulk of the police, who correspond to those which an English County Council controls. It is possible that these could be transferred to the control of the State Governments at an intermediary stage, provided always that a force competent to deal with political dacoity, anarchism and the like is reserved to the control of the Provincial Executive responsible to the Government of India. Provided that forces are retained strong enough to step in and restore order in the case of any break-down on the part of elective authorities, those authorities might be entrusted with the ordinary police work and large sections of the police during the transitional stage. An arrangement like this would enable Government to test the capacity of State Governments for maintaining order, before taking the final step of handing over the reserve or military police, including all the functions connected with the Criminal Investigation Department. When using the word police in these letters, I must be understood to mean reserve forces necessary and adequate to deal with political crime and to restore order under all conditions. But whenever the final transfer of this reserve force is made to elective governments in the major Provinces, the Government of India itself must then be made responsible to their electorates. The transfer of police to Executives responsible to electorates is tantamount to the consummation of responsible government, to the attainment of the final goal set forth in the Pronouncement.

In all federal countries the control of police is in the hands of the Provincial Governments. The Central Government has nothing to do with police, unless disorders are such as to demand suppression by troops, when the Central Government steps in. Indeed you may say that a great country is ripe for full responsible government, when in a sufficient number of provinces, electorates have been proved to be capable of maintaining order for themselves. From these provincial electorates a national electorate can be constituted fit to be trusted with the fullest responsibilities. I suggest, therefore, that a stage will be reached when the Imperial Government, judging by results ascertained by experience, will have to decide whether the electorate of this or that State can be entrusted with control of police. Whenever a sufficient number of State electorates have been given that control, then such electorates have been proved competent to form a general electorate to which the Government of India itself can be made responsible. It comes to this, that when control of all provincial functions, including police, can be given to electorates in the major provinces, then India is ripe for full responsible government. The transfer of police can only be made as the last preliminary, before the final change by which complete responsible government will be established. The changes by which electorates are made responsible (*a*) for all provincial functions, (*b*) for those of the Central Government, must come so near together as practically to be part of one operation. To speak of handing over all provincial functions, including police, to electorates is, in effect, to contemplate the consummation of the goal, the final establishment of India as a Self-Governing Dominion.

If this reasoning is sound, the Secretary of State is debarred from listening to demands that all provincial functions including police should be handed over, at this stage, to Executives responsible to electorates. He cannot accept such proposals, without transgressing the plain and explicit terms of the instructions by which he is bound. It is clear that the Imperial Government intends to transfer the responsibility for the whole government of India, which now rests on the British electorate, to Indian electorates as soon as may be. It is equally clear that it sees no electorates at the moment on whom that responsibility can be laid. It intends to develop such electorates, and to prove their strength, before laying on their backs the final function of government. I am sure that no British Parliament will consent to transfer the control of police to electorates, before they have seen what the electorates are going to be and have gauged their capacity.

As personally I believe that Parliament is right, I will not shrink from giving my reasons for that belief. Such limited electorates as there in India have never been exercised in responsibilities outside the narrow field of Local Government. To take those electorates, or any others which can be framed on paper, and to place upon them at one stroke the basic responsibility of maintaining order, would, in my judgment, expose India to the very disasters which have overtaken Russia. It is not the damage to life and property of which I am afraid, nor even the danger to the British position in India, for England was never so strong as she now is. My principal reason is that the one thing which can seriously postpone the achievement of responsible government by India is a catastrophic break-down of responsible government at the outset. Responsible government can, I believe, be achieved in measurable time by a process of evolution. In my judgment it can only be delayed indefinitely by revolution, by civil war, or a general break-down of public order. I am weighing my words when I say that continuous progress towards responsible government can only be delayed by subjects who try to undermine order, and by rulers who shrink from the duty of enforcing it.

It is for this very reason that I am slow to accept the view, held by a section of my own countrymen, that provincial functions cannot be transferred to electorates by instalments. An electorate, it is urged, cannot assume any political functions entrusted to the Provincial Government, without assuming the whole. The fifth proposition affirmed in the Joint Address—"that during the period of transition, governments "of two types must co-exist, the one responsible to "electorates for specific powers, the other to the Secretary of State for all other powers"—is challenged and denied. Have these critics realized the practical results of their own position? It means that a full and final responsibility for all political functions, including the maintenance of order, will sooner or later have to be placed, practically at one stroke, on electorates trained in nothing but the details of district, village and town administration. These electorates are to be confined to responsibilities in the sphere of local government. They are to be given no political responsibilities; and yet we are to look forward to a time when all the political responsibilities of India are to be placed on their backs together. It is just this which has happened in Russia, and the results are before us.

The idea that electorates can be trained for the discharge of political functions in the narrow sphere of district, village and town administration, is in my judgment a pure illusion. Whatever the text-books may say, they were not so trained in England. In the time of Cromwell the principle of election in Local Government was practically confined to small and narrowly restricted groups in the boroughs, which contained only a fraction of their population. In the

Parliamentary elections responsibility was confined to a minority so small that it was in fact an oligarchy. The circle of voters has been gradually broadened downwards, until, under the recent Act, it will, I am told, include a little more than one-fourth of the whole population.

My own short official experience in England and South Africa related for the most part to Local Government. As a political student I have seen something of Local Government in most parts of the British Commonwealth. Like the liver in the human body, local authorities are the least satisfactory organs in the body politic. The details with which they deal do not, unhappily, attract and evoke the best talent, either in administrations, or in electorates. The best men do not in practice come forward for election. It is also notorious that in all countries a lamentably small proportion of electors record their votes at the poll. I have seen the condition of local bodies in India adduced as conclusive proof of the inherent unfitness of Indians for any form of responsible government. Well, all I can say is that, if a political student were to test the capacity of Americans for self-government simply by a study of their local and municipal bodies, he would infallibly come to the conclusion that here was a people incapable of governing themselves. You will not evoke or develop whatever latent capacity for self-government there is in India, until you have imposed on electorates the burden of deciding such issues as are now decided, and can only be decided, by Provincial Governments. At present those Governments decide all the great questions at issue between Hindus and Muhammadans. Real political training will not have been started, until you have remitted some of these questions for settlement to executives and legislatures responsible to electorates including Hindus and Muhammadans. The great sections into which Indian society is divided must be exercised in the practice of settling these issues for themselves. The mere administration of Education and Municipal laws made over their heads, will never afford this training. Electorates must have power to pass laws for themselves, which determine the relative positions of Hindus and Muhammadans, and of their respective scripts and languages, in the educational and municipal system. But to give this process of training a chance, the existing Governments must stand by, with all their experience, and with all powers necessary, to maintain order. To jeopardize order at the outset is to jeopardize the whole prospect of developing electorates such as will presently be able to maintain order for themselves.

Those, I submit, are the conditions recognized and prescribed in the instructions under which the Secretary of State has been sent to India to seek for advice. It is those conditions which the system outlined in the Joint Address attempts to meet. Apart from extremists on both sides who honestly reject the Pronouncement, all agree that full powers of Local Government should now be devolved on district, village and municipal boards. The Joint Address proposes to go one step further. It notes that the existing Provinces, developed as satrapies of a vast Dependency governed from England, include populations the size of great European Nations. It proposes that the Governments of these vast areas should devolve instalments of political powers on units commensurate with the self-governing Provinces of the other federal countries, upon the model of which it is now proposed to develop the Government of India. That devolution it is proposed to increase, as the new Provincial State Governments and their electorates show their capacity for bearing the burden, until they have shown themselves able to legislate on and administer all functions of government including police. When that point is reached, it is recognized that the time has come when a new Constitution for India must be framed, under which the Government of India itself must be made responsible to the joint electorates of India.

Some better way of doing this than that suggested in the Joint Address may easily be found. I myself suggested in a letter to Mr. Bhupendra Nath Basu, which has since been published, that the best way might be to establish a responsible Executive for each existing Province, to which functions might be handed over by the old Provincial Governments, as the new electoral authority showed itself able to take them. After studying the mass of criticism that was made on this proposal, I came to the conclusion that smaller units were needed as the States of a future United States of India. That may or may not be. But when we are told that the method of specific devolution in India must be confined to district, village and town boards, and to such administrative details as can be devolved on local bodies, but that it cannot, by any manner of means, be extended to Provincial and political functions, I confess I view such arguments with reserve. Moderates who advance them have not, I feel, faced the consequence of their own reasoning. They do not see that, sooner or later, they are proposing to hand over at one stroke all political functions, the whole Government of India, to electorates which have never been called upon to exercise any responsibility, or to decide issues, in the genuine field of politics.

Really the crux of the whole problem lies in finding some plan, whereby instalments of real political responsibility can be placed on electorates, in order that their strength may be developed and proved, before they are asked to undertake the fundamental function of government, the maintenance of order; and where they are ready for that, they are ready for the whole government of India. It is therefore vital that a plan should be found, whereby some provincial functions can be placed in their charge, before they are asked to undertake them all. The public will do well to distrust arguments directed to prove that a thing obviously dictated by common sense cannot be done. I am old enough to remember in the nineties a Committee of Treasury officials who proved that old-age pensions could not be established in England. I have lived to see them established. I have heard the most experienced politicians demonstrate that the Union of South Africa was impossible. I have seen it accomplished. The truth is that in all such matters the difficulties lie, not in immutable facts, but rather in the minds and hearts of men, which can be changed, and need but the courage of a leader to change them.

XII

PRINCIPLES OF REPRESENTATION.

The first step in the path of reform must of course consist in the passing of an Act of Parliament, defining what the reforms are to be, and how effect is to be given them. In defining electorates two courses can be followed. They can be defined in the Act; but, as pointed out in the Joint Address, this course is likely to lead to a dangerous delay. The alternative is to remit the task of defining electorates to Commissioners appointed under, and named in, the Act. The most we can do now is to suggest principles upon which they should be based. To begin with, it is clearly important that the voters should, so far as possible, belong to the class who will feel the incidence of new taxation imposed by the men they elect. My own belief is that any fresh burdens, however imposed, will mainly fall on the land. How far the tenants are rack-rented already, I do not know; but in so far as they are not, it will be open to the landlords to transfer the tax to the cultivator by increasing the rents. I would therefore suggest the cultivation of a certain minimum area as the basis of the rural franchise. Nor, would I urge, should any voter, otherwise qualified, be rejected on the ground of illiteracy. Speaking of my own village in England, I would trust the political judgment of a small holder who could not write his name, more than I would that of the schoolmaster imported from London. In India you have, in the British officials, an admirable machinery for recording an illiterate vote, because they stand outside the issues which will divide parties. If necessary, enough of them can be drafted in from outside for the purposes of the election. Due weight can be given to the educated voters through university representation, or the representation of graduates.

In the initial stages of the experiment, the framing of the voters' rolls should be kept in the hands of the Provincial Government. The system should be designed, so far as possible, to make it clear that the legislature of each State is designated, by every possible means, as the body of citizens who are the ultimate trustees of the interests transferred to the State Government. I would leave it open to the Assembly to extend the franchise by legislation, which would be subject to the safeguard of the veto. But I would also leave it open to the Government of the Province to extend or improve the electorate, in case it should develop exclusive tendencies It is desirable to enlarge electorates, so far as possible, if only because they are then less easy to corrupt. The existing microscopic electorates are a standing invitation to corruption which it is most difficult to discover. I know of a case in another province, in which Rs. 30,000 was spent by an unsuccessful candidate for the Provincial Council.

The next step would be to delimit the constituencies; and this must be done largely with reference to population. So much the larger number of the constituencies will be rural that it would be well to give representation to Universities, or, where there are none, to residents with degrees. Avoid, if you possibly can, separate constituencies based on religious divisions. More than anything else, they will hamper and delay the development of responsible government in India. Proportional representation is the obvious remedy. The complexity lies only in the counting of the votes, which can be done by skilled officials. The voting is simple, and, after a period of trial, the electors will begin to realize that the results reflect the real divisions of the electorate. In this, as in other matters, understanding will come with experience, if only the opportunity of experience be given.

I have stated elsewhere that in several matters my advice was not taken by the signatories to the Joint Address. Communal representation is a case in point, and I am here at liberty to state my own convictions on the subject. Communal representation as I understand it means that Hindus and Moslems are to vote in separate constituencies, in such manner that a Moslem voter must vote for a Moslem candidate. He may not vote for one of any other religion; and the same applies to any other community to which communal representation is accorded. Moslems will thus learn to depend on an artificial protection, instead of facing the real source of their weakness, their relative backwardness in education. It is like keeping in irons a weak but healthy limb, which only needs exercise to recover its strength.

The concession of this principle when electoral institutions were inaugurated a few years ago, is the greatest blunder ever committed by the British Government in India. I believe that, if this principle is perpetuated, we shall have saddled India with a new system of caste which will eat every year more deeply into her life. So long as it remains, India will never attain to the unity of Nationhood. The longer it remains, the more difficult will it be to uproot, till in the end it will only be eradicated at the cost of civil war. To enable India to achieve nationhood, is the trust laid on us; and in conceding the establishment of communal representation we have, I hold, been false to that trust.

The system has eaten into the life of this people so deeply that, already, it is not possible to abolish at one stroke what might have been refused a few years ago. But I feel that we shall be guilty of an unpardonable crime against India if we fail now to make provision whereby these fetters, in which we have allowed her to bind herself, can be loosed.

The experience of America in the matter of slavery may help to a solution. When the constitution was framed, it was laid down that the importation of more slaves from Africa was to cease in a particular year; I think in 1808. And the slave trade ceased in that year. But the courage of the convention failed them in the matter of slavery itself; and no time was fixed after which slavery should cease to stain the soil of America. The result was that eighty years later slavery was abolished, but only by drenching that soil with the blood of a million men.

I plead this precedent for a definite time-limit to be set in the matter of communal representation. India is tied and bound by the chain of her past. Our first duty is to help her to break that chain instead of allowing one generation to rivet it more firmly than ever on those who come after. The least we can do is to fix a time-limit after which any arrangements now made for communal representation shall expire. Then we may hope that meanwhile the people of India may have learned such trust in each other that minorities will not insist on a system fatal to the development of all national life.

These, I know, are hard sayings for the Moslem community; yet "faithful are the wounds of a friend." Things there are bitter in the mouth, that chewed, swallowed and digested are sweet in the belly.

In the criticisms levelled against the Joint Address, it has often been urged that, before suggesting that electorates should be made responsible for certain functions, we are bound to say what the electorates are to be. This criticism, however specious it may seem at the first glance, will not bear the test of analysis.

To begin with, the Joint Address, like the Pronouncement of the 20th of August, relates, not to conditions in one Province, but to those of all India. It was not possible to compile schedules of voting qualifications appropriate to all the varying conditions of the several Provinces. I do not believe that such information at present exists in the files of the Home Department itself.

To this the answer may be made that discussion of the whole question should be postponed until the information is available, and all the suggested electorates can be described. But this criticism shows a misconception of the elementary conditions under which an electoral system must be framed. You cannot appoint officers to make an electoral system in the air. You must give them instructions. You must first tell them the principle upon which the vote is to be given. That principle, if our reasoning is right, is simple. *It is that the voters should be those who will in fact feel the effect of the votes given.* It follows, therefore, that the officers appointed to frame the electorate must also know what powers, legislative as well as administrative, the Governments responsible to the electorates are to exercise, and especially what their powers of taxation are to be. And these powers will differ in the case of each Province,—so various are their conditions and levels of advancement. In practice the definition of electorates is the last step, and not the first, in the framing of a Constitution

The first step, and the only one possible at this stage, is to think out clearly the elementary principle upon which the electorates are to be framed. With what objects in view are electorates to be brought into existence? Our answer is clear and precise, and is so stated for the purpose of criticism and discussion. The object in view should be to fit the voters placed on the list for the exercise of wider political responsibility, for which purpose we contend that some such responsibilities must be given them at the outset. They will certainly make mistakes, and it is only by making mistakes, and by suffering brought on themselves, that they will learn.

Granted an acceptance of that principle, the details can be worked out. Some of them can be settled in an Act of Parliament. Such an Act can enumerate the maximum powers that Parliament is prepared to transfer at the outset, in some Provinces more, in others less But the definition of the powers to be given to each Province (especially those of taxation) of the electorates and of all other details required for the perfecting of the constitution to be given to each of the new electoral Provinces, must be left to Commissioners charged to enquire and decide on the spot. Otherwise the Bill will break down before it reaches the Statute Book, or else there will be a long and dangerous delay—dangerous because, until this question is settled, India, not knowing what her future is to be, will remain in a state of ferment and unrest.

Upon this subject the words of the Joint Address itself may be quoted.

> The new pronouncement was only made on the 20th of August last, and the Secretary of State has reached India within three months from that date. It is utterly beyond the power, even of skilled and experienced officials, to collect within that time the facts and figures necessary before the details of proposals can be worked out. Nor, we venture to predict, will the Secretary of State himself be able to do this, with all the assistance which the Government of India can give him. The short time at his disposal here will be more than occupied with the study of principles, and if any attempt is afterwards made to work these principles into a complete scheme in London, we believe that it will fail for lack of detailed information, which can only be obtained on the spot. Such failure will mean delay, and delay will not be understood in India. It will surely breed distrust and continued agitation. The greatest need of India is that prompt and unmistakable steps should be taken to give effect to the policy outlined in the recent pronouncements. The only way in which this can be done, is by the early enactment of a measure by Parliament such as will set in train the progress of India towards responsible government there foreshadowed.
>
> The solution of the problem, we suggest, will be found in the precedent set by the Government of London Act of 1899. By this measure it was proposed to abolish more than forty vestries, and establish in their place a far smaller number of municipal bodies. The whole scheme, including the constitution of the new bodies, was firmly outlined in the measure. Yet the Parliamentary draughtsman, situated as he was in the middle of the subject dealt with by the measure, with all the forces of the Local Government Board, the Home Office, the London County Council, the City of London, and the Vestries at his disposal, was unable to cope with the innumerable details which had to be worked out before effect could be given to its provisions. In order to bring the new bodies into existence, it was necessary to delimit areas, fix the number of members on the various bodies, adjust their finances, and disentangle and re-arrange a multitude of details. All this was remitted to three Commissioners named and appointed under the Act. The moment the

Act was passed the Commissioners got to work, and, as their arrangements were framed, legal effect was given to them by orders in Council issued in terms of its provisions.

We believe that the adoption of this course is the only way to avoid a delay which will prove mischievous in the extreme to the peace and interests of India. It is not delay in bringing into being the new organs of Government that we fear. That of necessity is a task the details of which need time for their execution. Any attempt to burke those details will only end in further postponement. The delay, we fear, is in framing a measure which the Imperial Government can adopt for submission to Parliament, and in the passage of that measure into law. The trust of India in Parliament is unimpaired, and if once the scheme of reforms is firmly outlined in statutory form, and Commissioners are appointed to give effect to it, the people of India will not be found wanting in patience. Their energies will, we think, be devoted to aiding the Government and Commissioners in working out the details and carrying them into effect.

We agree, therefore, in advising that the specific points to which our agreement relates, and the outlines of the scheme sketched in these proposals, be laid down in an Act of Parliament: but that all questions, within those outlines relating to franchises, constitutions, powers, finances and such like details be remitted to not more than five Commissioners named under the Act, to be dealt with in India by the Commissioners, in consultation with Governments and People, the arrangements of the Commissioners, to be given the force of law by Orders in Council.

XIII

THE QUESTION OF AN UPPER HOUSE.

In the memorandum prefaced to the Joint Address it is suggested that the State legislature should consist of one Chamber only. No second Chamber was suggested, though I knew that a demand would be made for one to consist either of the largest land-holders, or of members elected by land-holders. The reason is that their hereditary pride revolts against the thought of seeking the suffrage of an electorate. The feelings of a zamindar are those of Coriolanus. But the effect of a landed Upper House will be to make the Assembly a House of lawyers and money-lenders. There will be constant collisions on the subject of taxation between the two Houses, and consequent deadlocks, as in Australia. The whole thing is too cumbersome for Provincial government. Besides, the land-holders, whose position gives them administrative experience, are badly needed in the Assembly. It will be, or should be, the dominant House; and if they are to serve their country, and do justice to their order, they must come to face the ordeal of popular elections. But something can be done to ease the process. On the London County Council the door is opened to a most useful class of members by the following expedient. Two-thirds of the members are directly elected. These members then co-opt another third. Now, if this expedient were adopted, the older land-holders would put up the younger members of their order and support them at the direct election, in order to secure seats for themselves by co-option. If induced to take part in elections, they will tend to become better and more indulgent landlords. They will, moreover, be driven to educate their sons for political life. If once the land-holding class be given the motive and opportunity of taking part in active political life, they may well work the salvation of India in its progress towards responsible government. An excessive artificial protection of any class invariably leads to its enfeeblement and undoing. Muhammadans, as well as landholders, will do well to reflect on this truth.

I understand that, at present, an agreement exists between representatives of the Hindu and Muslim communities to give 30 per cent of the seats to the latter. If it is decided to give effect to this concordat, the following arrangement might be considered Let us suppose that forty out of the sixty members have been returned by proportional representation. If the voting were strictly on religious lines, the result might yield thirty-three Hindus and seven Muhammadans. There would then remain the twenty members to be co-opted. Of these thirteen might be co-opted by the Muslim members, and seven by the Hindu members, the total result thus yielding the artificial proportions in the legislature laid down in the agreement. But Indians will have made a long step towards responsible government when they can trust each other so far as to forego such arrangements.

XIV

EXECUTIVE FUNCTIONS.

In order to sketch the constitution of the executive, it is necessary first of all to consider the functions which the new Governments would have to discharge.

These may be divided into two classes.

I.—In the first place there are the administrative functions which may involve legislation from time to time. Education is an instance. In this connection it is important to note that, under the existing system, educational policy is embodied in executive resolutions and regulations. Under a system of responsible government, it will have to be embodied in Education Acts passed by the Assembly. A change of policy will involve a legislative amendment of the Education Act.

II.—In the second place there are the legislative functions, those which involve making some change in the existing laws, which may or may not involve administrative action or change as well. The legalisation of marriages between castes might or might not involve some change in the machinery of registration.

As functions belonging to class I involve expenditure, a fairly complete list of them can be framed by reference to the estimates of the existing Provinces. From these estimates I will endeavour to frame a schedule showing the functions which could be transferred from time to time to the State Governments, leaving a residuum, when the process is completed, which will have to go to the Government of India.

Obviously the first powers to be transferred must be those the details of which have already been entrusted to the District and Municipal Boards.

These are—

I.

Vernacular education.
Medical relief.

Rural sanitation.
Veterinary aid.
Roads, other than provincial trunk roads.

The above is the smallest group of functions which could be transferred to the new bodies. I now come to those which might be added, either at once, or severally from time to time, as the administrative record of the new Governments may warrant. Nor is it necessary to transfer the same function to every State; for their conditions will differ. As we saw in the case of the Police, parts of one function can be transferred, leaving the rest for subsequent transfer. Certain forest areas, for instance, could be handed over, the Provincial Government reserving control of the rest. The following is a list of such functions:—

II.

Provincial trunk roads and bridges.
Agriculture.
Co-operative credit.
Factories and industries.
Museums and archaeology.
Registration of deeds.
Local railways.
Forests.
Irrigation.
Charitable endowments.
Famine relief.
Higher education.

Thirdly, we come to functions, which would only be transferred to a State when its Government and electorate had proved itself equal to the full burden of responsible government.

III.

Law and Justice.
Court of Wards.
Jails.
Police (final control).
Control of the district officers.

When this final transfer had been made to all the States, the old Provincial Government would vanish. Some or all of the following functions would then revert to the direct control of the Government of India :—

IV.

Irrigation systems included in the areas of two or more Provincial States.
Ecclesiastical affairs.
Archaeology.
Relations with Feudatory States.
Territorial and political pensions.
Ports and pilotage. (In the Presidencies.)
The Boards of Revenue.

With reference to this last item, there is something to be said hereafter.

XV

STRUCTURE OF THE EXECUTIVE.

The elected members having been returned, the Chief Commissioner would convene them and they would proceed to complete the Assembly by co-option. The Chief Commissioner would then send for the member whom he judged to be most capable of commanding the majority of votes and entrust him as Premier with the task of forming a Government. Let us suppose that the functions entrusted to the new Government are those in the first list, together with the control of municipal government, provincial trunk roads and agriculture. These functions would require the following portfolios:—

Primary education.
Local government.
Agriculture.
Public works.
Finance.

The Premier would select four colleagues from the Assembly, assign one of these portfolios to each of them, retaining the fifth for himself. And, if he were wise, he would do all this in friendly consultation with the Chief Commissioner. The Government having been constituted, they would meet the Assembly under the presidency of the Chief Commissioner. A speaker would be elected, and the Chief Commissioner would then withdraw.

As the methods of responsible government are strange to this country, it may be as well to explain one side of their working. Ministers, having been appointed, discuss their business and come to decisions amongst themselves in Cabinet, a word which does not appear in the formal constitution. These executive decisions are then brought to the Executive Council, a formal body of ministers over which the Chief Commissioner would preside. The decisions become operative when signed by the Chief Commissioner. Provided they are legal, he *must* sign them on the advice of the ministers. But, before doing so, a constitutional Governor is at liberty to discuss them with his ministers. Responsibility and the power of decision rest with ministers; but they are only too glad to consider the advice of a Governor who stands aloof from all parties and has perhaps watched the workings of government under several Administrations. Having often been in contact with Governors and ministers in the self-governing Dominions, I can testify to the cordial relations which prevail between them. Ministers often regard the Governor as their best friend and adviser. He, on the other hand, generally refers to "my ministers" in a tone of affectionate enthusiasm. In the situation I am sketching, responsible government in India would begin with an advantage which has been usually wanting in the Colonies. The Chief Commissioner would be an expert, with a thorough grasp of all the public affairs of his Provincial State. His instructions would make it perfectly clear that all control and all responsibility in respect of functions transferred to ministers rested with them, and not with himself. His experienced advice would be at their disposal, and, just because they were free to reject it, they would be all the more willing to seek and to consider it. His experience could influence them to the full. Responsibility would rest with them.

As the point was raised and gave serious trouble elsewhere, it should be laid down that the Chief Commissioner must not ratify any decision which the law officers of the Provincial Government advise him to be contrary to law. Otherwise he must sign, if, after hearing his advice, ministers are unable to change their decision, unless he is prepared to dismiss them and find others to take their place. He should be able to dissolve the Assembly only on two conditions—

(1) that he can find ministers who will take the responsibility of advising a dissolution, and
(2) on instructions from the Government of the Province.

The policy of ministers at the opening of a session would, in accordance with the ordinary tradition, be announced in the Chief Commissioner's speech. But the usual conventions should be dropped, and phraseology should be used such as would make it clear to the electorate that the decisions announced were those of their own ministers and not those of the Chief Commissioner. He should appear merely as reporting the decisions of the ministers, like an impartial Chairman reporting the resolutions of a Committee.

The Chief Commissioner, assisted by the Junior Commissioner, would continue to discharge the duties at present associated with his office (other than those transferred to the ministry) as an officer of the Provincial Government. In that capacity he would control the district officers as at present. He would, thus, be well situated to act as a link and a buffer between the officers of the old Government and the new. He would be able to mitigate friction between the district officers and those of the ministry, just as these officers themselves have done in their capacity as Chairmen of the District Boards and Municipalities. He would want his ministry to succeed, and would use his authority with his district officers to get them to smooth difficulties away. But those officers should be specifically divested of all responsibility for functions transferred to the ministry. The discovery which the electors will make, however slowly, that their own ministers are responsible for these things, and that it is through their members that they must seek relief, is the most important item in their education. For the sake of the electors district officers must be warned to decline specifically to touch grievances which come within the jurisdiction of the State ministries.

It may be useful to trace the manner in which the first ministry would assume its functions. Ministers would not take over their functions, until they had organized departments for the purpose. Aided by the Chief Commissioner, each minister would select a head of his department from the ranks of existing officials. Aided by that officer he would obtain the necessary subordinates from existing cadres, and so organize his department. When ready to do so he would notify the Provincial Government that he was prepared to assume control of the functions assigned to him. To take one example, the Educational Department would then transfer the whole control of primary education to the Minister of Education and to his new Department, built up from materials recruited in the old one.

Transfer of Officers.

In the Joint Address it is proposed that the transfer of officers from the Provincial staffs to those of the States should be arranged by ministers with the assistance of the Chief Commissioner. In the event of any final difference of opinion, the last word is to be with a permanent Civil Service Commission. The success or failure of the experiment will, I believe, largely depend upon the ability of the first ministers to secure as the permanent heads of their departments the ablest members of the existing Services. Decisions must rest with responsible ministers, but it is thus, and thus only, that ministers will have before them the best technical advice upon which to decide.

The estrangement developed of late years between educated Indians and members of the Service is deplorable. Like all such estrangements, it is largely due to ignorance of each other, and to want of any regular sphere of work common to both. It is safe to say that two classes of men never work together without coming to think better of each other. The Transvaal Civil Servant was the target of almost as much criticism and abuse as members of the I.C.S. are here. One Boer leader just before assuming office as a Minister, said in a public speech, that, of all the plagues from which the Transvaal had suffered, the plague of experts was perhaps the worst. Yet soon after he assumed office he confirmed the position of nearly if not quite all the British Heads of Departments under him. Most of them still retain those positions and speak of him in terms of the highest praise as a political chief. With the new ministers this was the rule, not the exception, and the reason was simple. They felt their own want of experience in technical matters. They wanted to succeed, and so like sensible men they put their prejudices in their pockets, and kept the men who knew the technical details. And before these men had worked together many weeks the mutual prejudice began to evaporate, and made room for mutual confidence and respect.

British officials, it may be said, will not serve under Indian Ministers. I can only say that several of them, and those not the least able I have met, have assured me that this would not be so. They have before their eyes the position in which British officials have served from the first under Egyptian Ministers. As one of my friends in the Service said, it would be a great adventure to him to throw his energies and knowledge into the task of making responsible government a reality in India. Any one, he added, could administer the village on lines worked out by men like Monro, Elphinstone and Colvin. It is easy enough to continue the methods whch they evolved and applied. To their successors of the present day is presented a new and far more delicate problem, and one calling for qualities higher than those demanded by the simpler conditions of the past.

And while we are on this point let me notice that the one real objection brought by Nationalists against this scheme is that the I.C.S. will thwart the work of the State ministries, with the deliberate intention of bringing them to naught, and so seeming to prove their incompetence. Those who use this argument fail to see that it is fatal to any scheme of reforms. If the assumption they make is correct there is nothing before India but revolution. Believe me, it is not correct. The charges you bring against British officials here, should really be directed against us, the people of England. It is we who have failed since 1858 to revise instructions which have long been obsolete. The members of the Service now have their instructions, and will be found loyal to their spirit as well as their letter. I venture to predict that as they realize the nature of the new enterprise before them, they will come to glory in its pursuit. There are many unofficial Europeans, who would feel more hopeful of this adventure, if their imaginations allowed them to depict the first Indian Ministers selecting as their permanent assistants, able members of the I.C.S. and of the collateral Services.

XVI

LEGISLATIVE POWERS.

We may now consider the manner in which the legislative powers of the States are to be defined. They cannot, like the executive powers, be scheduled at present. In framing a federal constitution the greatest difficulty to be faced is usually that of drawing the line between the legislative powers to be exercised by the Provincial Governments on the one hand, and by the National Government on the other hand. The only true guide is experience, and the best way in which to evoke and crystallize that experience is the device of enabling legislation, promoted by the provincial authority, and passed into law by the central authority. It was thus that the powers of the great municipal corporations of England were built up in the 19th century. Cities, like Manchester, Newcastle, and Birmingham had corporations based upon Charters granted centuries ago. In the first decade of the 19th century the introduction of steam power and the factory system caused an unprecedented growth in their populations, and created all sorts of needs which were not foreseen when the original Charters were granted. Such cities, for instance, required to be drained in accordance with modern sanitary science. This involved an interference with private rights and a power to raise loans, which was not within the existing powers of the Town Council. In order to obtain these powers, the Council would present a petition to Parliament in the form of a private Bill, in the clauses of which were defined all the necessary powers of expropriation, of making bye-laws and of raising loans. Such Bills, after passing their first and second readings, as a matter of course, were then referred to a Standing Committee appointed to deal with all measures of this class. The Corporation was represented before the Committee by counsel. Opponents of the measure would appear in the same way. Government departments would also be represented. Evidence would be heard for and against the Bill as a whole, and also with reference to its various provisions. The Committee would then report whether the Bill ought to be passed, and, if so, with what amendment of its original terms. In practice the Committee's report was practically decisive and was accepted by Parliament. In this way the Corporations obtained enabling legislation based on an experience of their actual needs and adapted thereto by an accurate and searching inquiry into the subject-matter to which each measure related.

Then came the period when the multifarious results of such legislation all over the country were reviewed by the Local Government Board, and consolidated into one Municipal Corporations Bill, which, when passed by Parliament, applied to all the great Corporations alike.

The powers, and especially the legislative powers appropriate to States, might well be worked out by some such process. And in doing so India might loose the heaviest fetters in which she has bound herself.

I have often heard it said that, before Indians ask for political powers, they ought first to devote themselves to the task of social reform. If Englishmen will think of the social reforms effected in their own country, they will realize how unfair and impossible a condition this is. What great social reform has ever been effected in England without legislative action? How could the employment of women and children in industries and mines, the status of married women, or the sale of liquor, have been reformed without the enactment of a new law?

In India the need for social reform largely arises from customs which have been crystallized by decisions in the courts, under the rigid legal system which we ourselves introduced from the West. The possibility of improving custom by custom has been checked in the process. But the necessary corrective, a legislature which could alter the binding effect of legal decisions, has been largely wanting in India. Before the Government will consent to alter the social law by statute, the reformer has been asked to convince the Government that he is backed by "an overwhelming demand" of public opinion. At present the means of showing that such a demand exists are wanting. On the other hand, the forces of reaction have every opportunity of convincing the Government that a change in the law will be followed by serious trouble. A desire to avoid trouble has become a dominant motive of Government in India. The social results are deplorable. In the Transvaal the marriage of a negro with a European woman, that is to say, between two castes, is contrary to law. In England I have often heard South Africa branded as the one country beneath the British flag in which marriage between any two sections of British subjects was forbidden. What was my surprise then, on coming to India, to find that under the law of that country no legal marriage between members of two different castes could be solemnised!

On glancing through the records of the Imperial Legislative Council for the year 1912, I came across a Bill moved by Mr. Bhupendra Nath Basu to allow civil marriage between members of different castes. The Bill, it seems, came to no more than this, that people might avail themselves of the Special Marriage Act of 1872 (which seems to provide for civil marriage) *without first declaring "that they profess no known religion in India."* With one exception, the debate was conducted exclusively by Indian members. That exception was the Home Member, who bluntly announced that, until the mover could show that there was an overwhelming preponderance of opinion in favour of the change, Government would oppose his measure. Mr. Gokhale pleaded in vain that the Bill might be allowed to go to a Select Committee upon which official members were in the majority. The mover, after replying, was supported by ten other members.*

* Their names deserve to be recorded:—

The Hon'ble Raja of Dighapatia.
,, Mr. Sinha.

With the majority against him, the whole corps of British officials were ordered by the Governor-General and his Council to march into the lobby and vote the measure down. So far as the British Government was concerned it might not even pass to be considered by a Select Committee before it was rejected.

Let Englishmen ask themselves what great social reform could have passed in their own country, subject to the condition that its promoters must, in some undefined way, show an overwhelming majority in favour of the measure before the Government would permit it to pass. Some reason might be found for requiring an overwhelming majority in the case of a reform like the total prohibition of liquor, which means depriving individuals of a freedom they already possess. But the case in question is one exactly opposite to this. As things are, two members of one religion, if belonging to two different castes, of which there are thousands, cannot contract a legal marriage without a formal and public renunciation of their religion. It is not enough for Government that their religious organizations have ample powers of excommunication. A couple effecting such a marriage would, as a matter of course, be outcasted, just as divorced Catholics upon remarriage might be excommunicated by their church. In India, such persons must themselves formally renounce their belief in their own religion before the State will extend to them the rights of civil marriage. A more flagrant interference with the liberty of conscience it is difficult to conceive. But Government will not permit its removal until it can be shown that "an overwhelming" preponderance of public opinion is in favour of the change. An overwhelming majority of Hindus must be shown to have consented, before two of them may contract a civil

The Hon'ble Mr. Haque.
,, ,, Gokhale.
,, ,, Madholkar.
,, ,, Madge.
,, ,, Dadabhoy.
,, ,, Jinnah.
,, ,, Bhurgri.
,, Sir V. D Thackersay.

marriage without first renouncing their religion. What business has Government to enforce the ordinances of the church against the enjoyment of civil rights, and those of the most elementary kind ? It is for a religion to enforce its own ordinances by its own sanctions, which in India are of the most powerful kind. And, as I have said already, no means are given to the reformer for testing public opinion.

The attitude of Government in India on these subjects confronts social reformers with obstacles which are heart-breaking. Their feelings may be judged by the following extract from an article by Mr. H. U. Divatia, M.A., LL.B., in the Bombay *Political Reformer* :—

> While it must be said to the credit of the British administrators of India in the sixties and eighties of the last century that they were sincere and eager to help the educated minority in their struggle to be free from what they believed to be unjustified social and religious trammels by permissive legislation, the same cannot be said of latter-day administrators who have betrayed an utter want of sympathy with the ideals of educated India and have shown themselves very reluctant to yield to the demands of educated Indians for further permissive measures, with the growth and change of public opinion. Witness, for example, the position of the Government towards the Minor Girls Protection Bill of the Hon'ble Mr. M. B. Dadabhoy. With the growth of education and progressive ideals in the country, the demand of social reformers for permissive legislative measures is bound to be more frequent and insistent and the Government would certainly be ill-advised if its dislike towards the aspirations of educated India were allowed to come in the way of social reform legislation, about the necessity of which the intelligent classes of the people themselves are the best judges. There are many rules of the Hindu Law in the domain of marriage, inheritance, joint family, stridhan, guardianship, maintenance, etc., which are found to be antiquated and unsuitable to the present stage of Hindu society, and it is by means of State interference only that reforms in this direction can be achieved. The demand must, indeed, come from the educated classes, but the Government should not adopt an indifferent attitude and bar the way of social progress. Some of

the other demands for legislation on social reform questions are as follows:—(1) Free and compulsory primary education as preparing, among other things, a ground for the promotion and spread of social reform schemes; (2) legislation for the protection of minor girls. A Hindu Marriage Act declaring the marriages between the different castes and sub-castes of Hindus, permissible and legal; (3) raising the age of consent to 14 or, if possible, to 16 years. This list is not exhaustive, but it represents some of the principal and pressing problems of the day, and it is hoped that Government will boldly encourage a policy of social progress and give effect to the articulate voice of educated India.

Government is not really standing apart from the struggle between conservatism and reform in India. As things are, the whole dead weight of governmental inaction is left to rest in the scale of conservatism against reform. In practice Government can only cease from this negative intervention by creating Indian electorates, and leaving their representatives to assume the burden of social reform; and this, I suggest, can be done in the most cautious way possible

A Nationalist leader asked me how the matter would work out under the proposals I am now making. And he pointed his question by suggesting an instance. There are, as he told me, a number of endowments left for specific purposes connected with temples. But no machinery exists for ascertaining whether the funds are actually applied to the purposes intended by the original donor. Under these circumstances, I suggested, the reformer would inaugurate a movement in favour of application by his State Government for powers to deal with the matter. A motion would be moved in the Assembly in favour of applying for such powers, and there the whole question would be publicly ventilated. If and when the motion was carried, ministers would then frame a petition to the Provincial Government in the form of an enabling Bill, defining the limits within which the Assembly might legislate on the subject. The Bill would come before the Provincial legislature, where the subject would again be discussed, and the Bill might then be referred to a Committee. The State Government would appear before the Committee by counsel. So would the trustees of the endowments, and any other parties concerned to support or oppose the measure. Evidence would be taken on questions of fact, and, in the process, the whole subject would be elucidated from top to bottom. The Committee would then report, giving their opinion whether the Bill should be passed; if so, with what amendments; and whether the other States of the Province should be allowed to adopt its provisions. Upon this report the Provincial Government would act within their discretion, with the fullest possible information before them. The Bill would be negatived, or passed with or without amendment. But, if passed, the enabling Act would define with precision the limits within which the State Assembly could legislate on the subject. It would then be the business of the courts to decide whether any measure passed by the Assembly, and any action taken thereunder by ministers, came within the powers defined by the Act. But the enabling Act itself would effect no change in the social law. The actual change would be effected by subsequent legislation passed by the Assembly, a representative body, within the limits of the powers provided by the enabling Act.

Let us now take the more serious case instanced above, that of the marriage law. Suppose that a State applied for powers to legislate on the subject, opponents of the measure might argue that the law of marriage was not a provincial but a national question, and ought to be reserved to the Indian legislature. They could point with force to the confusion which has arisen in America, by reason of the fact that the law of marriage was left, under the constitution, to the States. Counsel in charge of the enabling Bill might reply that, under the American constitution, Congress is forbidden to touch the subject. It has no overriding power of legislation whereby to harmonize the marriage laws of the 48 States. In India it is not proposed to deprive the central legislature of power to deal with the subject. Such powers might therefore well be conceded to the States, so that each might be free to liberalize the law within its own jurisdiction. Later on, when public opinion had expressed itself through the action of various Assemblies, the Central Government would be free to review the situation, and introduce a statute harmonizing marriage law for the whole of British India.

With these arguments before it, the Provincial Government, which is but a branch of the Government of India, and under its orders, would be able to decide whether the powers sought were such as a State Government could properly exercise, or whether they ought to be reserved absolutely to the Indian legislature.

By the use of this method, State Governments could also be encouraged to devise and suggest new sources of revenue for themselves. Ministers might think that revenue could be raised by a stamp on patent medicines sold within their jurisdiction, and submit the proposal to the Assembly. That body, having approved of the principle, would instruct the ministry to apply for enabling powers to the Government of the Province. The ministry would then frame an enabling Bill for submission to that Government, which would, of course, be fully informed as to the views of the Government of India. The arguments of the ministry and of the interests affected would be heard, and the enabling Bill would either be rejected, or passed with or without amendments. But if passed, it would constitute a permanent addition to the powers of the State. Within those powers, as defined by the Provincial Act, the ministry would proceed to frame a taxing measure of their own, which, when passed by the Assembly, would come into law. If the results, when tested by experience, proved satisfactory, the powers of the enabling Act might then be extended to all the others, to be exercised or not, as might be determined by their own discretion.

Thus, in the course of years, by the fullest public inquiry, and by actual experiment, the powers, which a State needs and is capable of exercising, would be worked out. Whenever the time arrived for summoning a convention to frame a constitution, under which the Government of India would come to be responsible to an Indian Parliament and electorate, that convention would have before it ample materials for determining what powers should finally vest in the State Governments, as distinguished from those which would have to be reserved to the Parliament of India.

XVII

CO-RELATION OF PROVINCIAL AND STATE GOVERNMENTS.

The character and working of the new system proposed has now been outlined with sufficient clearness to enable us to consider what changes should also be made in the structure of the existing Governments of the Provinces.

I take it, as a matter of course, that half the Executive Councils would be Indian. But these Indians, I would urge, should be promoted officials. The popular leaders will all be wanted for the State ministries, and the great corps of Indian officials should be encouraged by having these posts opened to them. In the terms of their appointment, I would make it emphatically clear that the Indian members of Council hold office on exactly the same tenure as their colleagues. and are, like them, responsible to the Secretary of State. Each Member of Council, moreover, should have an alternate to take his place automatically in case of illness or absence.

The Governor, I suggest, should, if possible, be a man who has served as Governor of a self-governing Colony. One of the greatest difficulties to be faced in the transition stage is the absence of knowledge which exists amongst all classes in India of the meaning and practice of responsible government. It is vital that the heads of the old Provinces, who will largely control the transition, should bring such experience from outside. Of experience in the technique of Indian government they will find an ample supply on the spot. But something ought also to be done to provide members of the Indian Civil Service with the experience which their present position denies them. The Imperial Government might with advantage arrange that, in future, the Private Secretaries of Colonial Governors should be seconded from the junior ranks of the Indian Civil Service. Such men would return to India with ideals other than those which their present training provides. It is not less important that in future Colonial Governors should be drawn from the senior members of the Indian Civil Service. They would thus get an actual experience of the working of responsible government, and could then be drafted back to act as the Chief Commissioners of States in India. The self-governing Colonies would, I believe, if properly approached on the subject, welcome the chance of offering themselves as a training ground for those who are to superintend the extension to India of the system under which they have thrived. The arrangement would help to create a new and better understanding between the different parts of the Commonwealth.

In considering the reform of the Legislative Councils of the old Provinces, it is well to hold in mind that, under the system proposed, they would be organs of government which are vanishing quantities. The present Governments of the Provinces will continue to exist only as trustees of residuary powers to be handed over as rapidly as possible to the elective Governments of the States, or, finally, to the Government of India, when it becomes answerable to an Indian electorate. It would exist to maintain order in the period of transition, and whenever the States are ready to assume that basic function, it would vanish. In the meantime it cannot be too clear that, in the discharge of its temporary functions, the Government of the Province is responsible to the Secretary of State, and has all the powers necessary for discharging the duties laid upon it. But in doing so it should be exposed as strongly as possible to the influence of Indian opinion. In all its executive acts, and in any legislation which it may find it necessary to pass, it should be exposed to the fullest criticisms of an Indian Assembly. In order to meet these conditions, the Governor-in-Council should legislate by ordinance. But the draft of every ordinance, and the estimates in draft, should come before a Provincial Council composed mainly of delegations from the States, together with some non-official members appointed by Government. The official voters would disappear from the Council altogether. The Government would be represented in debate by the members of the Executive Council and their alternates. Seven or eight spokesmen are amply sufficient for the conduct of debate. But the officials should not vote. The Council should be free to discuss and pass any recommendations it chose, whether on matters of principle or detail. The final action of Government, whether in legislation or in the allocation of public funds, would only be taken in the light of such recommendations; but the power of final decision would rest with the Government. The enabling Bills of the States, for instance, would all come before the Council; but Government would nominate a majority on the Committee to which such Bills were referred, leaving the Council to elect the minority. The Council formed of delegations from the State Assemblies would constitute an important link between their Governments and that of the Province, until it had disappeared.

The Treatment of Friction.

Whatever powers are conceded from time to time to State Governments, I would strongly urge that they should be conceded outright, subject to the power of veto on legislation, which, in the transition stage, should be exercised by the Provincial Government, not by the Chief Commissioner. The latter should be protected, as far as possible, from occasions for friction with ministers. The Provincial State Governments will be kept within their statutory powers by the action of the courts, which would be competent to decide whether any legislative provision or executive action was *intra vires*.

Friction there will be under this or any other scheme. There is serous friction at present between the Official and elective members of the Legislative Councils. Under some of the schemes proposed the friction would be such as would certainly burst into flames. The scheme proposed in the Joint Address aims at developing a feeling of responsibility in electorates by making ministers and assemblies directly answerable to them for definite duties, and that this responsibility may be clear, as well as to reduce friction, it is proposed that the electorates should have separate officers and revenues of their own. But even so the separation will still be imperfect. Government is one, and all its functions are interconnected; though to say that they cannot be separated enough for the purpose of delegation to different authorities is contrary to facts before our eyes.

Let us take an example which has often been raised in the course of the last few weeks. The Police controlled by the Provincial Government are convinced that sedition is being taught in a school controlled by the State ministry. They ask ministers to take such action as is taken at present. Ministers refuse, and a deadlock occurs.

In passing, let us notice that exactly the same position can arise, if District and Municipal Boards are given real control over schools. But leaving that aside, it is not difficult to suggest provisions whereby difficulties of this kind can be overcome. It might be provided, for instance, that all such matters should be raised in the first instance with the ministry, by the department, and not by the Governor-in-Council. If the ministry and department cannot agree, then let the case be remitted to a joint session of Executive Councillors and Ministers in equal numbers, sitting together as a board of conciliation, under the chairmanship of the Governor, who should not vote or take sides unless called upon to do so as umpire. If the joint meeting fail to agree to an order, then let an order be made by the Governor. The sovereign specific for friction is to have some machinery for settling questions. Open questions are open sores.

XVIII

SELF-TAXATION.

As a scheme for developing responsible government, its success or failure would, I believe, largely depend upon the procedure whereby the transfer of fresh powers and revenues to the State Governments is to be effected. To start with, the States must have their full share of the revenues, that is to say, a share equivalent to what has been spent on the functions assigned them in past years, and this share must grow with the general growth of the Provincial revenues. But the basic facts of Indian finance are these. For the last century the British Government has steadily reduced the proportion of unearned increment from land due to the public treasury. Hence the failure of that Government to break down illiteracy in India. Crores and crores of rupees are necessary for that purpose, but they can only be raised by governments responsible to the people themselves. It is in facing that burden of self-taxation, and by no other means, that the people of India will achieve responsible government. The newspaper *Sanjiwani* raises its hands in horror at the proposal:—'This plan of leaving 'to Provincial (State) Governments certain specific 'powers of taxation would make such Governments 'unpopular.' * This is perfectly true, and many Governments will perish in the process, until at length the electorates have learned that no ministers can remain responsible to them for discharging their orders except in so far as they make themselves responsible to ministers for discharging the cost. Responsibility is always two-edged. The whole virtue of the system is that it brings home the elementary lesson that men can only reap as they have sown: and that way lies the making of men. The pace at which India

* See issue of November 22.

will travel towards the final goal will mainly depend upon how soon this difficult lesson of self-taxation is learned.

Hence the importance of periodic settlements of standing revenues. The States must be given an ample share of revenue at the outset. But if the question of increasing that share is left open from year to year, it is human nature that ministers should direct all their energies to obtaining more funds from the Provincial Government, for the extension of their services, instead of facing the unpopular expedient of fresh taxation. The energies of the new bodies will be spent in a chronic squabble with the old. The only remedy is for Parliament, or its agent the Secretary of State, to settle the matter on the advice of Commissioners reporting direct to itself for a period of years, revising the settlement by the same method at the end of that period. It is not fair to leave the onus on the Government of India and its Provincial Governments. In dividing the revenues between themselves and the popular Governments they cannot escape the charge of loading the dice. But if every seven years the settlement is revised by an impartial authority reporting direct to the Secretary of State, Governments of each type will then know what they have to spend, and each will realize that fresh taxation must be faced, if it wishes to increase its programme. I say, without fear of contradiction, that neither this nor any other Government in India will break down illiteracy which will not face fresh taxation.

Sanctions.

The finances of the State Government should be subject to audit by an officer appointed by the Provincial Government, whose reports should be published. On questions of extravagance or of expenditure made without proper authority, the auditor would report to the committee of public accounts appointed by the Assembly. The auditor should have full powers of holding an inquiry, wherever he sees traces of corruption. The Provincial Government might have power to bring delinquents to trial, in default of action taken by the ministry. The auditor would have power to disallow expenditure which was *ultra vires*: but a power of remitting a surcharge should vest in the Provincial Government.

The borrowing of money would of course require the sanction of the Provincial Government, but otherwise I would urge that all sanctions in detail should be avoided. The necessity of obtaining sanctions in detail is a certain cause of friction. Let the new authorities be given a perfectly free hand, within the powers conferred upon them, if only that the responsibility which rests upon them may be perfectly clear to their electors. For details, let Government rely on the influence of the Chief Commissioner with his ministers. Let the one check be a power of total suspension, in cases where a State Government has clearly and absolutely failed in the duties imposed on them. If a Government so misuses the powers with which it is charged as to produce disorder, the Government, upon which rests the final duty of maintaining order, must have a power of suspending the delinquent authority and of acting in its place. But in such cases the Chief Commissioner should always change places with one in another State. He should never be exposed to the charge of aiming at personal rule. Summary suspension would of course require the sanction of the Government of India, subject to confirmation by the Secretary of State, and would only take place in the event of public disorder due to the action of the State Government.

It should be settled, I suggest, at the outset, that, after seven years' trial of the system, a Commission should be appointed by the Secretary of State to examine its results. The Commission should include men who had served as Governors of self-governing Colonies and of Crown Colonies. The Commissioners should be asked to examine the record of each State, and advise whether further powers should be transferred to it, and, if so, what those powers should be. In the case of any State which had utterly failed in its task, it would be open to the Commission to advise a reduction of powers, or else total suspension. Responsible government will progress far more quickly if administrations saturated with corruption, or paralysed by inertia, are suspended, as those of Native States have been under similar circumstances. The old Government would then step in, to purify and reinvigorate the administration, until conditions seemed ripe for a further essay in responsible government. But, except in the case of public disorder, such suspension should only take place on the recommendation of such a Commission as that suggested above.

I believe this power of suspension, if made a reality, will do more than anything to accelerate progress towards responsible government, because it will embolden Parliament and Secretaries of State to insist on a free extension of further powers to States which are showing a real capacity for self-government. The most paralysing influence in India at present is the conscious weakness of Government. It is taken as an axiom that no forward step can ever be retraced. The inevitable result is that Government shrinks from any forward step, or deliberates so long that the step is obsolete when taken. These timid advances, moreover, afford too little scope for latitude in the various provinces of this diverse country. The reforms suggested are too rigid and too uniform for the multifarious conditions. The secret of rapid progress is, wherever a community shows capacity for progress, to enable it to move forward as quickly as it can. To do this Government must make experiments, and proceed by trial; but it is useless to talk of experiments, unless you are prepared to retreat where failure is ascertained, as well as to advance where success is proved. There would be more than twenty States in India. It is greatly to be hoped that at the end of seven years a marked addition could be made to the powers of many of them. No general unrest would be caused by suspending an egregious failure which was casting discredit on all the rest. And each of these Governments would always have fresh prizes before it to be gained, until the final reward of complete responsible government had been reached. The principle of specific delegation gives all the elasticity, which is wanting in the various schemes so far suggested.

The powers of the States would thus be built up in two separate ways. The known executive functions of Provincial Governments would be scheduled. To begin with, an instalment of those powers would be entrusted to States, and every seven years the question of transferring further powers would be deliberately considered in the light of the record achieved by each electoral authority.

Side by side with this periodic transfer would go on a continuous transfer of new legislative powers, sought, as the need might be felt, by the States from the old Provincial Governments, acting as the agents of the Government of India. The limits of those powers would all be defined with accuracy in the terms of enabling Acts. From time to time the Government of India would review these local Acts, and generalize their contents into laws applying to all the States, the general Acts repealing and taking the place of local Acts. In this manner would be gradually built up the constitution of a self-governing India, on the one solid foundation of experience.

In conclusion, I desire to affirm once more the conviction which underlies the whole of these detailed suggestions. The backward and defective state of education in India is a reproach to the British Administration which must be wiped out. An improvement and extension of teaching in all its branches is a vital necessity. But that of itself will not avail to prepare Indians for the task of responsible government. On the contrary, it will prove to be a danger and positive mischief, unless accompanied by a definite instalment of political responsibility. It is in the workshop of actual experience alone that electorates will acquire the art of self-government, however highly educated they may be.

There must, I urge, be a devolution of definite powers on electorates. The officers of Government must give every possible help and advice to the new authorities, for which those authorities may ask. They must act as their foster-mothers, not as their step-mothers. But if the new authorities are to learn the art of responsible government, they must be free from control from above. Not otherwise will they learn to feel themselves responsible to the electorates below. Nor will the electorates themselves learn that the remedy for their sufferings rests in their own hands. Suffering there will be, and it is only by suffering, self-inflicted and perhaps long endured, that a people will learn the faculty of self-help, and genuine electorates be brought into being. The control to which the District Boards have been subject has, in my judgment, almost destroyed the benefit of the experiment inaugurated by Lord Ripon.

I am proud to think that England has conferred immeasurable good on India by creating order and showing Indians what orderly government means. But this having been done, I do not believe the system can now be continued as it is, without positive damage to the character of the people. The burden of trusteeship must be transferred, piece by piece, from the shoulders of Englishmen to those of Indians in some sort able to bear it. Their strength and numbers must be developed. But that can only be done by the exercise of actual responsibility steadily increased, as they can bear it. It cannot be done by any system of school teaching, though such teaching is an essential concomitant of the process.

The goal now set by the recent announcement of the Secretary of State will only be reached through trouble. Yet troublous as the times before us may be, we have at last reached that stage of our work in India, which is truly consonant with our own traditions. In the past our work has been that which other great Empires have accomplished. We may well be glad to feel that in our generation has begun the work of remodelling the Government of India on those principles which all free nations have borrowed from England, and which most of them have now combined to defend at immeasurable cost. No human work is perfect, but the foundations of responsible government in India have been firmly laid by our predecessors. Yet finer qualities will be needed in raising the walls; and the task is one worthy of this epoch in our history, if only because it calls for the effacement of ourselves.

APPENDIX I.

MEMORANDUM BY MR. P. C. MITTER.

Keeping myself within the twelve points agreed upon, I note below anoutline of the form of government I should like to have. I should like to mention at the outset that the twelve points agreed upon by the signatories were certainly not a scheme of reform, but were meant to be mere outlines on the basis of which it was desired that schemes of reforms might be discussed.

TERRITORIAL REDISTRIBUTION.

This is referred to in Article (2) of the points of agreement. I suggest that we should begin by redistributing the provinces on a linguistic basis provided the people concerned do not oppose such a territorial redistribution. I suggest the following redistribution:—

(1) *The Punjab and Sindh* to form one province for the reserved government For the transferred Provincial State I would prefer to have the Punjab and Sindh as two separate States. If, however, the people of Sindh do not like to be separated from Bombay or do not like to be formed into a separate State for transferred powers, I would not recommend any redistribution. The Punjab and Sindh

(2) *The United Provinces* —From the present administrative area of the United Provinces I would exclude the eastern portion speaking the Bhojpuri language (the language of the present western portion of Behar, south of the Ganges). By eastern portion I refer to the districts of Benares, Gorakhpur, Mirzapur, Azamgurh, Ballia and Gazipur. The populat on of these districts is about 4 millions. It would perhaps be desirable to add a small Hindi-speaking area of the Central Provinces to the altered United Provinces. The population of the United Provinces as altered will be about 43 millions instead of its present population of about 46 millions. The United Provinces.

As regards the Provincial State for the United Provinces, for the reserved powers I would for the present leave the same administrative area unless there be a demand by the people to form themselves into one or more Provincial States. If Mr. Curtis's ideas about subdivision into small Provincial States really embodies a political truth, then the people themselves in the course of the next seven years will realize their difficulties, and at the time of the next septennial enquiry they themselves will ask a subdivision into Provincial States. If on the other hand it is attempted to force this political truth upon an unwilling people, then the resentment and the bitterness created by such forced subdivision will not give the people concerned a fair chance of realizing as to whether Mr. Curtis's suggestion embodies a political truth or not. The United Provinces State Government.

(3) *Behar.*—As already stated, I would include the six eastern districts of the United Provinces and the north-eastern portion of the Central Provinces (Hindi-speaki g). Behar then will be a fairly compact province speaking practically the same language. I would exclude Orissa from Behar, and also the district of Manbhoom and the subdivisions of Deoghur, Jamtara and Pakaur of the district of Sonthal Pergannas on the ground that this small area is practically Bengali speaking. The population of Behar will then be about 35 millions. The addition of the six rich districts from the United Provinces will, it is expected, minimize Behar's financial difficulties. Behar.

I would have the same area for the Provincial State for Behar unless there be a strong demand by the people concerned for subdivision into two Provincial States. Behar State Government.

Bengal.

(4) *Bengal.*—To the present area of Bengal I would add the district of Manbhoom and the subdivisions of Deoghur, Jamtara and Pakaur of the district of Sonthal Pergannas. There is a fairly wide-spread demand for the inclusion of the district of Sylhet (at present forming part of the province of Assam) into the province of Bengal, but on the other hand an objection has been suggested, namely, that if Sylhet be excluded from Assam, Assam's position will be financially unsound. I would leave it to the Commissioners when they come out to decide the question of inclusion of Sylhet into Bengal. The population of Bengal including that of Manbhoom and the small portion of Sonthal Pergannas will be about 47 millions. An objection has been suggested that the population is too large. I would, however, point out that the population of the province of Bengal as it was constituted after the first partition was 57 millions and odd, and that population consisted of three linguistic areas, viz. the Bengalee, the Ooriya, and the Beharee. Regard being had to the insistent feeling on the question, I would strongly urge the inclusion of this outlying small area within the province of Bengal.

Bengal State Government.

For the Provincial State of Bengal I would have the same area. The observations I have made while discussing the question of subdivision of the United Provinces apply to Bengal with much greater force. As a Bengalee I can assert with confidence that any attempt to subdivide Bengal will raise such bitter feelings that it will be extremely impolitic even to suggest a subdivision. As I have already observed, if after seven years' administration the Bengalees in the outlying districts feel that their affairs are being neglected, they themselves will ask for a subdivision.

Madras.

(5) *Madras.*—I would exclude the small Ooriya population of about a million and a half in Ganjam from the province of Madras and would put all the Ooriya-speaking population in one Provincial State. Excluding the Ooriyas, Madras has a Tamil-speaking population of about 16 millions in the tract known as Dravida, a Telugu-speaking population of about 15 millions in the tract known as Andhra and a Malyayali-speaking population of about 3 millions in the tract known as Malabar. It also includes a Canarese-speaking population in the tract known as Canara. The Canarese-speaking population however is divided between the provinces of Madras and Bombay Their total number is about 4 millions. I would like to place all the Canarese-speaking population under one administrative unit, and I would leave it to them to decide as to whether they would like to be included in the province of Bombay or in the province of Madras. In other words, when the Commissioners come out they should decide the question after consulting the public opinion in Canara, and after considering other pertinent questions that may arise. I do not discuss the total population of Madras as that will obviously depend upon the ultimate decision.

Madras State Government.

As regards the Provincial State of Madras, I leave it to the people concerned to decide whether they should start with one Provincial State or more. My own suggestion is to have as few changes as possible in the beginning.

Bombay.

(6) *Bombay.*—I would suggest the exclusion of Sindh from Bombay and the inclusion of the whole of the Mahratta-speaking population of the Central Provinces and Berar. As regards the Canarese-speaking population, I have nothing to add to what I have said in connection with that population in Madras. The question of the inclusion of the little State of Coorg, which adjoins south Canara, may perhaps be usefully left to the Commissioners. The Mahratta-speaking population of Bombay including Berar and a portion of the Central Provinces will be about 13½ millions, and the Guzratti-speaking population will be about 3½ millions.

Bombay State Government.

As regards the Provincial State dealing with the transferred departments, my inclination is to have the same area for both the Governments.

Orissa.—I would strongly urge that the whole of the Ooriya-speaking population of 6½ millions including a small tract from Madras should be formed into a separate Provincial State for the transferred powers. For the reserved powers the area so formed may be placed either under Madras or Bengal as the Commissioners may determine after consulting Ooriya public opinion. Orissa.

Form of Government—Reserved Powers.—I would suggest that all the above six provinces should be administered by a Governor brought out from England with an Executive Council of 4—2 Europeans and 2 Indians. The delegation of certain powers to Provincial States will require a re-arrangement of officers. In Bengal, for example, I would suggest that after the delegation of certain powers to the Provincial State of Bengal the Commissionerships of Divisions may be abolished, and so there would be sufficient work for four members of the Executive Council. I shall discuss the question of redistribution of officers later on, as that will obviously require a more detailed consideration. Government Executive Council.

I would suggest that an Indian member of the Executive Council should always be in charge of the Police Department. I would further suggest that the member in charge of the Police Department should have associated with him a Committee of three non-official elected members of the Legislative Council. All papers of the department should be available to these members and they should be freely consulted on all questions. If there is difference between the member in charge and the non-official Committee, the matter should be placed before the Governor in Council. Further, unless the Governor in Council unanimously decides to the contrary it would be open to the members of the non-official Committee to raise a debate in the Legislative Council, but the ultimate decision will rest with the Executive Government. It is well known to the authorities that there is a strong feeling amongst a large section of the people about Police administration. I will not discuss as to whether there is justification for this feeling or not, but in my view the existence of the feeling is a point which cannot be ignored. The Government has nothing to lose but everything to gain by allowing extended popular influence (I do not suggest for the present actual power) over the administration of Police Department. While I do not agree with those who ask for the immediate transfer of the Police Department to popular State Government, I strongly feel that extended popular influence will be conducive to the best interests of law and order and purity of administration. Suggestions about police department.

Form of Government—Transferred Powers.—I would suggest that responsible Ministers should remain in charge of the transferred powers. So long as the Ministers can command a majority, they should remain in office. There should be three to five Ministers according to the size of the Provincial State and to the number and importance of the delegation of departments. The Ministers should be whole-time men and should be paid reasonable salaries. Ministers of State Government.

Under the Ministers there should be permanent officials to be selected from the permanent Civil Services, Indian and Provincial. The officers so selected will be subordinate to the Ministers and will not be in any way subordinate to the Reserved Government, viz the Governor in Council. There should be a complete bifurcation of the services of the reserved and the transferred departments, but I will allow under certain conditions transfers of officers from the reserved to the transferred department and *vice versa*. Permanent officials of State Government.

Administration of the Transferred Government by Permanent Officers.—One of the most important departments which it is proposed to be transferred is the department of Local Self-Government. This department will obviously require permanent officials (*a*) to check and audit accounts, (*b*) to detect and check corruption if any, (*c*) to supervise with a view to the performance of statutory duties by local bodies, and (*d*) to reporting to the Minister in charge any neglect to initiate or to carry out local administrative measures in the interests of the health, sanitation or safety of the local public. For these and other incidental work I would have below the Minister in Local Self-Govt.—the officers of this department.

charge two permanent paid officials who will form a Board on the lines of the Local Self-Government Board in England. Immediately subordinate to these officers will be a permanent official in charge of an administrative division. For this post I should like to have an officer of the status and position of a first-class Collector. Subordinate to these officers I would have an officer in charge of the local bodies of each district. For these posts I should like to have officers of the status and position of Deputy Collectors of 10 to 15 years' standing. The staff suggested by me is by no means too large I am familiar with the conditions of my province of Bengal, and I desire to justify the staff proposed by taking Bengal as an illustration. Rural Bengal consists of about 67 thousand square miles, and as the whole of that area has to be mapped out into Village Union Committees, I expect the total number of such Committees will be something between 7 thousand to 10 thousand. Besides the 25 District Boards a fairly large number of Sub-district Boards or Circle Boards will have to be created. Besides all these there are a large number of Muffassil municipalities. Regard being had to the volume of work appertaining to such a large number of local bodies, the staff proposed by me is by no means too large.

Departments other than Local Self-Government

As regards other departments that may be transferred, *e g* departments like Agriculture, Forest, Co-operative Credit, and Economic Development of Provinces, Education, Sanitation, Excise, etc., they have already got their separate permanent staff and there will be no difficulty in transferring such staff bodily to the transferred department.

Abolition of Commissionerships of Divisions

Administration of the Reserved Government by Permanent Officials.—Here again I would draw my illustrations from the province of Bengal. As I have already stated, I would abolish the Commissionerships of Divisions I would also suggest the separation of judicial and executive functions. At the present moment Local Self-Government and the large amount of work relating to the subordinate magistracy occupy much of the attention of the Commissionerships of Divisions. Under my scheme, on account of the separation of the judicial and executive functions and of the transfer of Local Self-Government to Provincial State Government, it will be unnecessary to have a supervising officer of the type of a Commissioner of a Division specially as I have proposed 4 members of the Executive Council. Further, the abolition of the Commissionerships of Divisions will tend towards decentralization, and many questions will perhaps be decided far more expeditiously and satisfactorily if the District Officers are allowed to correspond and take their orders direct from the Provincial Government without the intervention of Commissioners of Divisions.

District Officer—his functions.

I shall now take up the question of district administration. If the District Officer be relieved of his magisterial duties and his duties relating to Local Self-Government his main duties will be his work as a Collector and his work as the head of the Police. After a District Officer is relieved of the duties mentioned, it will perhaps be not necessary to subdivide some of the districts in Bengal as have been proposed. This will mean a considerable saving to Bengal, and perhaps there are questions of subdivisions of districts in other provinces as well. In the next place, after the District Officer is relieved from the work of these two important departments it will, I hope, be possible for him to pay greater attention to the work of the supervision of his Police subordinates. This, I believe, will tend to the improvement of Police administration. Further, in small districts the District Officer will, I hope, be able to manage only with a Deputy Superintendent of Police and the number of posts of the District Superintendents of Police may in future be reduced.

Judicial Administration of the District.—Instead of there being two services of Deputy Magistrates and Munsiffs there may be one service of officers who will administer both civil and criminal justice with the District Judge as the head of the judiciary in the district. I have dealt with this question of a separate judicial service in my book on the Separation of Judicial and Executive Functions, and I have shown in that book by detailed calculations that a separate judicial service will ensure both economy and efficiency.

Reserve departments and transferred departments.

Departments to be Transferred to the Provincial State Government.—The condition of different parts of India not being the same, the departments to be transferred need not be the same. In a province like Bengal (and I take Bengal only as a type) I would suggest that all departments save and except (1) Land Revenue, (2) Stamps, (3) Civil and Criminal Justice, (4) Prisons, (5) Ports and Pilotage, and (6) Police, should be transferred; that is to say, the following departments will be transferred: (1) Local Self-Government, (2) Education (all branches including higher, secondary and primary), (3) Registration, (4) Agriculture, (5) Co operative Credit and Economic Development of the Province, (6) Forest, (7) Irrigation, (8) Sanitation, (9) Medical, and (10) Excise. The work of the Finance and the P.W. Departments will have to be apportioned between the reserved and the transferred departments. I shall illustrate what I mean. If a Police-station or a Court House has to be built, such building will have to be erected by a P.W.D., appertaining to the Reserved Government. If on the other hand a registration office or a dispensary has to be constructed, such building will have to be constructed by a P.W.D. appertaining to the Transferred Government. This will mean in practice that a number of officers of the P.W.D. will have to be placed under the Reserved Government and a number under the Transferred Government The same arrangement will obviously be necessary with regard to the Finance Department.

On what principle should departments be transferred or reserved.

The principle underlying the suggested arrangement about the transfer of the departments is that to start with departments on which the safety of the State depends should be reserved, but subject to extended popular influence (and not power). The departments mainly concerned with the building up of the people should be immediately transferred. Although I believe that in most Indian Provinces an intelligent electorate and also men fit to administer all provincial departments may be found, yet it is equally a fact that no opportunities have yet been given to the electorate or to the administrator It is possible therefore that through inexperience there may be some mistake or some error of judgment in the beginning. If departments concerned with the safety of the State are entrusted at the beginning and if mistakes are committed either by the electorate or by the assembly or by the ministers, then not only will the State suffer but the enemies of progress will take full advantage of such mistakes, and it is likely that our ultimate progress will be retarded rather than furthered by such enthusiastic attempt to take over the whole administration of the province. On the other hand, if my suggestion about the transfer of the departments be accepted even if mistakes are made, such mistakes will only affect the Indian interests mainly, and non-Indians and enemies to the progress of India on democratic lines will have less legitimate grievance against the responsible Government. Furthermore, the most important point is to create and develop a wide electorate. Once a wide and intelligent electorate is formed, progress is bound to come. Then again, I should like to point out that I have suggested many important safeguards about the most important of the reserved departments, viz the Police Department—I mean the safeguards about the administration by an Indian member and other points already mentioned. The transfer of the departments already mentioned is the maximum I desire for the present for provinces like Bengal. Obviously for small and backward provinces the transfer of functions should be less. Take the case of a poor and backward State like the suggested Provincial State like Orissa In that Provincial State, for example, I would suggest a transfer of the departments of Local Self-Government (including Roads and Bridges, Dispensaries, Sanitation, Primary Education and other functions usually administered by District Boards and Muffassil municipalities). The great problem in such a State would be to develop a proper electorate. Regard being had to the comparative dearth of men and money and the probable backwardness of the possible electorate, it will not do to transfer as many departments as may be suitable for Bombay or Bengal There may be other Provincial States in an intermediate state of progress. So the best course would be to prescribe in the amendment of the Statute a maximum and minimum of the departments to be transferred, leaving to the Commissioners when they come out to settle details after full enquiry and after taking evidence of the people concerned and of the Public generally.

Scheduled Districts.—I would suggest that all the scheduled districts should be administered by the Reserved Departments.

Revenue and its Division between the Reserved and Transferred Powers.—This is no doubt one of the most important and difficult of questions. I venture to think, however, that the solution is not as difficult as it seems to be. The chief apprehensions are—(*a*) that there would be constant friction between the Reserved and the Transferred Departments, (*b*) that it would be asserted that the Reserved Government would unfairly keep more revenue in its control, and would attempt to starve the transferred departments, (*c*) that such apprehended attempt would cause great discontent in the public mind, (*d*) that it would be difficult to formulate a machinery for equitable adjustment, and (*e*) that it would be difficult for the Responsible Government to raise revenue for the improved administration of the departments transferred without causing great discontent. I propose to meet the points raised. In the first place I would like to observe that it is proposed in the outlines agreed that the division of the revenue would be made by the Commissioners. So, to start with, we have an independent tribunal. I admit that the task of the Commissioners may be a difficult one I suggest that some time before the Commissioners take up the question of the allotment of revenue the Government should appoint a Committee of six—three officials and three non-official elected members of the Legislative Council—to report on an equitable division of the revenues of the Province. The points of reference should include—

(*a*) The total net revenue with a detailed statement of the net revenue of each of the revenue heads (*i e* heads in which the income exceeds the expenditure).

(*b*) The total net expenditure with a detailed statement of the net expenditure of each of the expenditure heads (*i.e.* heads in which the expenditure exceeds the income)

(*c*) The growth of revenue and of expenditure of each of these heads.

(*d*) The legitimate requirements of growth of expenditure of the departments reserved by the old Government with direction to report specially on any excessive growth of expenditure of any department due to abnormal conditions and the likelihood of such expenditure diminishing or remaining stationary, or growing still more. (As for example in Bengal the expenditure on the department of Police has grown by about 60 % during the last few years on account of abnormal conditions. The Committee may state their views as to whether this expenditure is likely to grow more, or remain stationary, or diminish).

(*e*) The legitimate requirements of growth of expenditure of the transferred departments with directions to report specially about departments like Education, Sanitation, Local Self-Government, Co-operative Credit, Agriculture and Fishery, that is to say, departments concerned with the moral and material progress of the people and the province.

(*f*) The contribution to the Government of India in the past, and what contribution would be necessary in the future.

The non-official members should be allowed to select a financial expert, and a staff under such expert, to examine all detailed papers. They should be allowed to select, with the approval of the Government, an officer or a retired officer of the financial department of the type of say Mr. Bhupendra Nath Mitter, C.I.E., or Mr. Kristolal Dutt. The report, together with the note of the expert, should be placed before the Commissioners, who should ultimately decide after taking any further evidence or making any further enquiries that they may think fit. It should be laid down in the statute that a percentage (to be fixed by the Commissioners) of the net revenue of the reserved departments (including the growing revenue) should be made over to the transferred departments. It should also be laid down that out of the growing revenue an additional percentage (to be fixed by the Commissioners) should be made over to the transferred departments. The reason for this last suggestion is that an examination of the finances will show that it will be possible to allocate an additional percentage to the departments dealing with the moral and material development of the people and the province. Further, if some additional percentage can be handed over, it will go a long way towards conciliating public opinion. Nor will this additional percentage jeopardize the financial necessities of the reserved departments. I would suggest a further safeguard in order to conciliate public opinion, namely that at the end of say every two years the reserved departments will hand over to the transferred departments 75 % of their surplus, keeping only 25 % for their own future use. In order that this provision may be an effective one, I would suggest the appointment of one or two Indian financial experts (of the type of officers already mentioned) to scrutinize the accounts of the reserved departments. These two officers (or one as the case may be) should be appointed by the non-official ministers with the approval of the Governor. They will have access to all papers and will report to the non-official ministers from time to time. The non-official ministers will have liberty to bring all cases of excessive expenditure to the notice of the Governor-in-Council, and will also have the right to raise a debate in the Legislative Council. The decision of the Legislative Council, however, will be treated merely as a recommendation, and the sole object of providing for such debate is to ventilate any particular question of expenditure before the public and to appeal to public opinion. The expenses of the reserved departments are more or less fixed—at any rate they ought to be so. I shall proceed to illustrate my Scheme with reference to some important heads of the Bengal Administration For facility of reference the figures are set forth in Appendix A It will appear from these papers that the total income of the reserved departments is Rs. 5,53,82,013 (five crores fifty-three lakhs and odd), and the total expenditure of the main reserved departments is Rs. 2,42,02,121 (two crores forty-three lakhs and odd). If we deduct from this the net imperial contribution of Rs. 2,06,26,341 (two crores six lakhs and odd) there remains a balance of one crore five lakhs and odd. A calculation will show that about 63 per cent represents the total expenses of the reserved departments and the imperial contribution, and about 37 per cent represents the balance. The Commissioners may therefore safely say that 35 per cent of the consolidated revenue should be handed over to the Provincial State Government of Bengal. Further, if we examine the figures about the growth of revenue and expenditure of the reserved departments we find that the growth of revenue in four years amounted to 53 lakhs 80 thousand and odd, and the growth of expenditure amounted to 32 lakhs 76 thousand and odd. This leaves a margin of 21 lakhs and odd in 4 years. An additional percentage (say 50) out of this margin of net growth may also be handed over to the transferred departments. The net result therefore would be that the reserved departments will not only have income sufficient to pay their expenses but a margin of several lakhs from each year's revenue, and a further margin out of the difference between growth of revenue and growth of expenditure. *The reserved departments therefore can have nothing to complain. The transferred departments also can have no legitimate grievance because I have suggested that the ultimate residue should go over to them. I have also suggested an independent tribunal and a scrutiny both before the matter goes up to the tribunal and also after.* I believe I have answered points (*a*) to (*d*) of the difficulties set out above. I should like now to consider point (*e*) and I propose to show, taking Bengal as my type, that there are possibilities of meeting additional expenses if the Responsible Government choose to incur such expenses for development of the province. The important spending departments of the Responsible Government will be (*a*) Local Self-Government, and (*b*) Education. I take up first Local Self-Government which has two important branches, viz. the District Boards and the Mofussil Municipalities. The total revenue of the District Boards from local rates, tolls and ferries is about 65 lakhs, and the total revenue of the mofussil municipalities (excluding the small contribution from Government) amounts to about 54 lakhs. If the Responsible Government desire to spend 25 per cent more on improvements they will have to spend about 29½ lakhs more on the head of Local Self-Government.

I now take up the question of expenditure on Education and note some of the principal items:—

Calcutta University	1,15,000
Direction	1,64.393
Inspection	9,33,936
Government Colleges (general) . ..	9,53.535
Secondary High Schools	5,96,721
Grants-in-aid	29,45,916
About	48 lakhs

(This is the gross and not the net expenditure I have not included here, for example, the receipt from fees, etc of the schools and colleges)

If a 25 per cent increased expenditure be estimated the amount necessary will be 12 lakhs.

I next take up the question of the expenses for introducing compulsory primary education. Compulsory primary education may be introduced into—

(i) the whole of the province, as also

(ii) into such towns and villages where the population is more than 1,000.

My calculations have been based on the present scale of expenditure and are for male children only. Further, I have taken into account only such areas where a literacy of 33 per cent already exists.

The additional amount necessary for the whole of the province will be about 50 lakhs, and that for towns and villages with a population of more than 1,000, will be about 9 lakhs. Assuming that the whole of this additional expenditure will fall upon the Provincial State Governments, the increase on this head will be 50 lakhs or 9 lakhs as the case may be.

I think, to start with, we should introduce compulsory primary education into towns and villages where the population is more than 1,000. The total expense on this head therefore will be 9 lakhs.

From the above it will appear that the total additional expense on the basis of 25 per cent increase in expenditure for Local Self-Government and Education will be about 50 lakhs.

How this Additional Expenditure can be Met.—I now propose to consider how this additional expenditure can be met. The suggestions contained in the following lines are mere indications of the possibilities of the situation and not cut and dried schemes which would obviously require further consideration. I would divide my suggestions into two heads—

(*a*) possibilities of increase of taxation, and

(*b*) possibilities of increase of income by development of resources.

HEAD (A).

Head of income.	*Present income.*	*increase.*
1. Sale of stamps .	62,96,051	3,14,000 (increase of 5 % suggested)
2. Sale of court-fee stamps	1,54,15,690	7,70,000 (increase of 5 %). and 2,00,000—about (increase of court-fee stamps from 1 anna to 1½ annas in petitions and petty litigation, and from 8 annas to 10 annas in important litigation).
3. Sale of demy paper	3,22,8[illegible]	3,22,885 (It is suggested that three papers should be sold for 2 pice instead of 1 pice)
		Total increase—about 16 lakhs.

Head of income.	Present income.	increase.
Excise ..	. 1,51,40,074	7,57,000 (5 % increase suggested.)
Registration	.. 18,12,868	1,81,286 (10 % increase suggested)
		Over 9 lakhs.
		Total—over 25 lakhs

Growing Heads of Revenue.—Most of the heads of revenue are growing. I note below two heads amongst many :—

1. I find in the report of 1915-16 (p. 16) that the current demand for cesses increased by 2,13,488 over that of the previous year, and in the report of 1914-15 (p.) that the increase was 1,89,607. I may take it that the average increase is about 2 lakhs

2. Waste land is a growing source of revenue. Waste lands let out under capitalists' settlement rules would yield an increase of about 1,50,000 (one lakh and a half) in two districts only. The figures as to waste lands settled to ryots are not available to me. This must yield a considerable increase, perhaps not less than 8 lakhs. Almost every head of revenue is a growing one.

Additional Cesses that may be Suggested.—A malaria cess of 1 pice in the rupee may be suggested. The assessment may be made in the same way as Road and P.W. Cesses are assessed. The total gross rental on which these cesses are assessed is 12 crores and 7 lakhs.

A cess of 1 pice to the rupee will yield 18 lakhs and 80 thousand rupees. This sum may be made over to the District Boards who are at present entrusted with measures relating to sanitation. I think this cess will be the least unpopular of all cesses. I desire to point out that most of the increase suggested by me is by indirect taxation. A young democracy should be very cautious about direct taxation. The only direct taxation I have suggested is the small figure of 1 pice per rupee for malaria. This tax will benefit the tax-payers immensely.

The sum total of the increase suggested above come up to Rs. 47 lakhs and 30 thousand. It very nearly approaches the total of 51 lakhs. The difference of 3 lakhs and 70 thousand will, I believe, be met from the other sources of growing revenue and the growth of the income from the settlement of waste lands.

Development of Resources.—I will now discuss the question of the possibilities of the increase of income by development of material resources. The material resources of the province can be very materially increased by judicious administration, and I note only a few of various possibilities.

Salt—

The total consumption of Bengal is—70,76,593 maunds.

The average price is—Rs. 3-6-2 per maund.
(The figures are taken from the report of the Salt Department).

Imports into Bengal—

Great Britian ..	..	..	24 lakhs maunds (neglecting thousands).
Portsaid	..	..	.. 24 lakhs maunds (nearly)
Spain	..	..	.. 15 lakhs ,, ,,
Massowa	..	..	.. 10 lakhs ,, ,,

At present the difficulty in obtaining tonnage is well known. Although the difficulty will be less after the war, yet for years some difficulty will continue. Further, trade in more valuable articles but of less bulk will be more attractive. My suggestion is that at any rate the approximate amount of 50 lakhs of maunds imported from countries other than Great Britian should be attempted to be manufactured locally This will mean saving in expenses in tonnage and will give employment to a large number of people uneducated and educated. The average saving to the Government will be, I understand, at least one rupee per maund The total income will be 50 lakhs if non-British salt be dispensed with, and will be 70 lakhs if British salt be also dispensed with The employment to a large number of people will mean greater trade to Great Britain and income to Government in tariff duties and income tax.

Cinchona.—At present less than ½ a square mile is under cinchona cultivation, and cinchona yields over 5 lakhs annually to Government. The area of the Darjeeling Sadar Sub-division is 726 square miles. I understand over 50 square miles are fit for cinchona cultivation. If cinchona cultivation be extended to about 10 square miles gradually, it will yield about 1 crore of rupees and will be of incalculable benefit to the malaria-stricken population of Bengal.

Reserved forest	..	4,871
Protected do	.	1,711
Unclassed do.	..	4,030
		10,612 sq. miles.

Forests.—The forests area of Bengal is 10,612 square miles. The total gross revenue from forests is 11,50,000. The gross income per acre is about $\frac{1}{64}$ rupee or about 1 pice to the acre. The price of pure milk is 4 seers or less per rupee (about double the rate prevailing in England), and of ghee is about 80 rupees to the maund. It is possible to develop the income of the forests (without any risk of deforestation) by providing large grazing grounds to reliable concerns It should not be difficult to set apart in various plots 2 to 3 thousand square miles suitable for grazing purposes and developing forest resources. The income on this head alone would in course of time rise very considerably.

Medicinal plants and materials for manufacture of paper may under suitable administrative methods increase the income of the forests very materially.

I hope I have discussed the question sufficiently to satisfy *prima facie* that the financial question will not stand in the way.

Electorates.—I desire to take up the question of Electorate next. The following figures relating to the Province of Bengal are interesting and helpful:—

Total population	..	..	45 millions (about)
Exclude females	..	..	22 ,, ,,
			23 millions (about)
Exclude those under 21	..	..	11 ,, ,,
Remaining male population about 21 years ..	..	..	12 millions
Total male literates	..	..	2,401,716
Do. in English	..	..	319,904
Ordinary cultivators (males)		..	8,190,142

I will now quote certain figures showing the number of cess-paying estates and tenures.

Total number of revenue-paying estates paying cess ..	..	..	..	102,272
Total revenue-free	..	..	..	30,378
Do. rent-free	..	..	..	38,578
Do. tenures assessed with cesses	..		..	2,393,124
		Total	..	2,564,352

Keeping in view the above figures I would suggest direct voting on the following lines for the Province of Bengal:—

(*a*) All persons paying a rent or revenue of Rs. 100 or cesses of Rs 6-4 whether literate or illiterate.

(*b*) All persons paying a revenue or rent of Rs. 16 or a cess of Re. 1 who can read and write vernacular or English with facility.
(*c*) All persons paying an income tax on an assessment of Rs. 2,000.
(*d*) All persons paying tax to a municipality on an assessment of Rs. 250 per annum.
(*e*) Do. on Rs. 50 per annum who can read and write a vernacular or English with facility.
(*f*) All literates in English who pay any rent, cess, or tax or who own any property valued at not less than Rs 500.

If the qualification be fixed on the above lines I expect that out of 2,564,352 cess-paying estates or tenures a comparatively small number will go out on the ground of illiteracy. These men are mostly middle-men and well-to-do ryots Literacy prevails largely amongst these people. If I allow a deduction of 10 per cent on the ground of literacy and a deduction of 30 per cent on the ground of low property qualification, I believe I shall be allowing an ample allowance. The total number will be 1,025,740 (little over a million). Many of these persons are middle-men, as also actual cultivators. Many of these persons are prosperous ryots. As regards 8,190,142 classed as actual cultivators, my estimate is that the actual number of voters will vary from 5 to 10 per cent of the total, *i e.* from 40 thousand to 80 thousand. In other words, the total number will be 1,025,740 + 40 thousand = 1 million 65 thousand, or 1,025,740 + 80 thousand = 2 millions 5 thousand. Besides the above there will be some income tax-payers or municipal tax-payers. I suppose we may expect about 1 million and 75 thousand voters out of a total male population of about 12 millions. The possibilities are far more satisfactory than the state of the Electorate in England long after the Reform Act.

Legislative Council.—I would leave the settlement of details to the Commissioners who would decide after considering various interests. I would like however to indicate the main outlines of the strength, power and functions of the Legislative Council. I suggest a total strength of about 125 to consist only of non-official elected members. The Council should have power to legislate, to tax and to pass the budget of the Responsible State Government. I would also give all powers which a Responsible Government usually possesses, but such powers should be within the limits of the departments handed over to the Responsible State Government.

A Second Chamber.—A Second Chamber, if constituted on right lines, would be a very useful brake, and I should like to have a Second Chamber for the Responsible State Government In the Second Chamber I should like to have a combination of men of intellect and of sober views, and men of outstanding position in the province, as also of men with large stakes in the country. I would suggest a body of the following type:—

(*a*) To be elected from the Universities 4
(No one to be eligible for this seat who has not served on the Senate for less than 10 years and is below 40 years in age).
(*b*) Non-official Europeans paying an income-tax of not less than 12,000 a year 6
(*c*) Non-official Indians paying an income tax of not less than 18,000 a year 4
(*d*) Zemindars (same property qualification as in the present Imperial Council election) 5
(*e*) By the Legislative Council 6
(*f*) All ex-Members of Executive Council who have permanent residence in the province .. ..
(*g*) All persons who served as Ministers of the Provincial State Government fo not less than 5 years .. ..
(*h*) All permanent ex-Judges of the High Court who are also permanent residents of the province .. .. ..

All legislations and resolutions of the Legislative Council will have to be passed by the Upper House. But a resolution or a legislation which has been thrice presented before the Upper House at an interval of 6 months each, will automatically become binding without any purther reference to the Upper House. The budget will be presented before the Upper House as a Financial Statement. All questions of taxation affecting interests of minorities or of special classes will have to be passed by the Upper House.

APPENDIX A.

TOTAL ACTUAL REVENUE OF THE MAIN HEADS OF REVENUE.

Land Revenue	2,98,96,600	
Deduct expenditure including charges of District Administration, Land Revenue collections, management of Government estates, Survey Settlement and Land Record	36,76,687	
(Reserved Department)		2,62,19,913
Stamps	2,24,37,340	
Deduct expenditure	5,82,710	
(Reserved Department)		2,18,54,630
Excise	1,51,40,074	
Deduct expenditure	7,28,506	
(Transferred Department)		1,44,11,568
Provincial Rates	....	2,33,854
(Reserved Department)		
Income tax	72,26,611	
Deduct expenditure	1,52,964	
(Reserved Department)		70,73,647
Forest	11,45,610	
Deduct expenditure	5,93,635	
(Transferred Department)		5,51,975
Registration..	18,12,868	
Deduct expenditure	11,27,328	
(Transferred Department)		6,85,540
Total actual revenue of the main revenue-yielding Departments		7,10,31,126
Total of Reserved Departments ..		5,53,82,013
Total of Transferred Departments		1,57,49,113
		7,10,31,126

TOTAL ACTUAL EXPENDITURE OF THE MAIN HEADS OF EXPENDITURE OF THE RESERVED DEPARTMENTS.

General Administration		23,88,887
Courts of Law	1,03,11,110	
Deduct income	8,48,999	
		94,62,111
Jails	25,06,667	
Deduct income	9,09,149	
		15,97,518
Police	1,09,03,783	
Deduct income	1,96,866	
		1,07,06,917
Ports and Pilotage	13,73,063	
Deduct income	13,49,562	
		23,501
Political	....	23,187
Total actual expenditure of the main heads of expenditure of the Reserved Departments		2,42,02,121

IMPERIAL SHARE.

Land Revenue	1,16,43,984
Stamps	1,12,18,670
Income tax	36,13,306
	2,64,75,960
Deduct net transfer from Imperial to Provincial	58,49,619
	2,06,26,341
Net income from the following main Departments, viz. Land Revenue, Stamps, Excise, Provincial Rates, Forest, and Registration	7,10,31,126
Net expenditure on the following Departments, viz. General Administration, Courts of Law, Jails, Police, Ports and Pilotage, and Political	2,42,02,121
	4,68,29,005
Deduct present contribution to Imperial Government	2,06,26,341
Net income available for the remaining Departments	2,62,02,664

SOME FIGURES RELATING TO GROWTH OF REVENUE.

				Net income.
Land Revenue (Reserved) ..	1915-16 ..	2,98,96,600		
	1912-13 ..	2,79,87,155		
				19,09,445
Stamps (Reserved) ..	1915-16 ..	2,24,37,340		
	1912-13	2,07,43,853		
				16,93,487
Excise (Transferred) ..	1915-16	1,51,40,074		
	1912-13	1,37,59,045		
				13,81,029
Provincial Rates (Reserved) ..	1915-16	2,33,853		
	1913-14	1,31,340		
				1,02,513
	(The figures of 1912-13 have not been taken because of the making over of 29 lakhs and odd to the District Boards in November 1913).			
Income tax (Reserved) ..	1915-16 ..	72,26,611		
	1912-13 ..	55,51,652		
				16,74,959
Registration (Transferred) ..	1915-16	20,36 068		
	1912-13	18,23,161		
				2,12,907
Total growth of Reserved Departments	53,80,404			
Do. Transferred Departments	15,93,936			
	69,74,340			69,74,340
Average for each year ..		..	..	17,43,585
Net decrease in Forest Revenue (Transferred) ..	1912-13 ..	16,00,601		
	1915-16 ..	11,45,610		
				4,54,991
				65,19,349
Average for each year ..				16,29,837

SOME FIGURES RELATING TO THE GROWTH OF EXPENDITURE.

			Net increase of expenditure.
Courts of Law	1915-16	1,03,11,110	
	1912-13	96,39,400	
			6,71,710
Jails	1915-16	17,75,645	
	1912-13	10,17,401	
			3,58,244
Police	1915-16	1,09,03,783	
	1912-13	83,99,859	
			25,03,924
			35,33,878
Deduct saving in expenditure in general administration			1,57,825
Net growth			32,76,053
Average for each year			8,83,469
Deduct saving in expenditure in general administration			39,456
Net increase			8,44,013
Net increase in expenditure without taking into account Police			10,29,954
Average for each year			2,57,488
Deduct saving in expenditure in general administration			39,456
Net increase excluding Police			2,18,032

SOME FIGURES RELATING TO SAVING IN EXPENDITURE.

			Net saving.
General Administration	1912-13	25,46,712	
	1915-16	23,88.887	
			1,57,825
Average for each year			39,456

APPENDIX II.

RESOLUTION adopted by the Thirty-First Session of the Indian National Congress held at Lucknow, on the 29th December, 1916, outlining a Scheme of Reforms as a Definite Step towards Self-Government. Also adopted by the All-India Muslim League at its Meeting held on the 31st December, 1916.

RESOLUTION.

(*a*) That having regard to the fact that the great communities of India are the inheritors of ancient civilisations and have shown great capacity for government and administration, and to the progress in education and public spirit made by them during a century of British Rule, and further having regard to the fact that the present system of Government does not satisfy the legitimate aspirations of the people and has become unsuited to existing conditions and requirements, the Congress is of opinion that the time has come when His Majesty the King-Emperor should be pleased to issue a Proclamation announcing that it is the aim and intention of British policy to confer Self-Government on India at an early date.

(*b*) That this Congress demands that a definite step should be taken towards Self-Government by granting the reforms contained in the scheme prepared by the All-India Congress Committee in concert with the Reform Committee appointed by the All-India Muslim League (*detailed below*).

(*c*) That in the reconstruction of the Empire, India shall be lifted from the position of a Dependency to that of an equal partner in the Empire with the self-governing Dominions.

REFORM SCHEME.

I.—Provincial Legislative Councils

1. Provincial Legislative Councils shall consist of four-fifths elected and of one-fifth nominated members.

2. Their strength shall be not less than 125 members in the major provinces, and from 50 to 75 in the minor provinces.

3. The members of Councils should be elected directly by the people on as broad a franchise as possible.

4. Adequate provision should be made for the representation of important minorities by election, and the Mahomedans should be represented through special electorates on the Provincial Legislative Councils in the following proportions:—

Punjab—One-half of the elected Indian Members.
United Provinces—30 %
Bengal—40 %
Behar—25 %
Central Provinces—15 %
Madras—15 %
Bombay—One-third

Provided that no Mahomedan shall participate in any of the other elections to the Imperial or Provincial Legislative Councils, save and except those by electorates representing special interests.

Provided further that no bill, nor any clause thereof, nor a resolution introduced by a non-official member affecting one or the other community, which question is to be determined by the members of that community in the Legislative Council concerned, shall be proceeded with, if three-fourths of the members of that community in the particular Council, Imperial or Provincial, oppose the bill or any clause thereof or the resolution.

5. The head of the Provincial Government should not be the President of the Legislative Council, but the Council should have the right of electing its President.

6. The right of asking supplementary questions should not be restricted to the member putting the original question, but should be allowed to be exercised by any other member.

7. (*a*) Except customs, post, telegraph, mint, salt, opium, railways, army and navy, and tributes from Indian States, all other sources of revenue should be Provincial.

(*b*) There should be no divided heads of revenue. The Government of India should be provided with fixed contributions from the Provincial Governments, such fixed contributions being liable to revision when extraordinary and unforeseen contingencies render such revision necessary.

(*c*) The Provincial Council should have full authority to deal with all matters affecting the internal administration of the province including the power to raise loans, to impose and alter taxation, and to vote on the Budget. All items of expenditure, and all proposals concerning ways and means for raising the necessary revenue, should be embodied in Bills and submitted to the Provincial Council for adoption.

(*d*) Resolutions on all matters within the purview of the Provincial Government should be allowed for discussion in accordance with rules made in that behalf by the Council itself

(*e*) A resolution passed by the Provincial Legislative Council shall be binding on the Executive Government, unless vetoed by the Governor in Council, provided however that if the resolution is again passed by the Council after an interval of not less than one year, it must be given effect to.

(*f*) A motion for adjournment may be brought forward for the discussion of a definite matter of urgent public importance, if supported by not less than one-eighth of the members present.

8. A special meeting of the Provincial Council may be summoned on a requisition by not less than one-eighth of the members.

9. A Bill, other than a Money Bill, may be introduced in Council in accordance with rules made in that behalf by the Council itself, and the consent of the Government should not be required therefor.

10. All Bills passed by Provincial Legislatures shall have to receive the assent of the Governor before they become law, but may be vetoed by the Governor-General.

11. The term of office of the members shall be five years.

II.—Provincial Governments.

1. The head of every Provincial Government shall be a Governor who shall not ordinarily belong to the Indian Civil Service or any of the permanent services.

2. There shall be in every Province an Executive Council which, with the Governor, shall constitute the Executive Government of the Province.

3. Members of the Indian Civil Service shall not ordinarily be appointed to the Executive Councils.

4. Not less than one-half of the members of the Executive Council shall consist of Indians to be elected by the elected members of the Provincial Legislative Council.

5. The term of office of the members shall be five years.

III.—Imperial Legislative Council.

1. The strength of the Imperial Legislative Council shall be 150.

2. Four-fifths of the members shall be elected.

3. The franchise for the Imperial Legislative Council should be widened as far as possible on the lines of electorates for Mahomedans for the Provincial Legislative Councils, *and the elected members of the Provincial Legislative Councils should also form an electorate for the return of members to the Imperial Legislative Council.*

4. One-third of the Indian elected members should be Mahomedans elected by separate Mahomedan electorates in the several Provinces, in the proportion, as nearly as may be, in which they are represented on the Provincial Legislative Councils by separate Mahomedan electorates.

Vide provisos to section I, clause 4.

5. The President of the Council shall be elected by the Council itself.

6. The right of asking supplementary questions shall not be restricted to the member putting the original question but should be allowed to be exercised by any other member.

7. A special meeting of the Council may be summoned on a requisition by not less than one-eighth of the members.

8. A Bill, other than a Money Bill, may be introduced in Council in accordance with rules made in that behalf by the Council itself, and the consent of the Executive Government should not be required therefor.

9. All Bills passed by the Council shall have to receive the assent of the Governor-General before they become law.

10. All financial proposals relating to sources of income and items of expenditure shall be embodied in Bills. Every such Bill and the Budget as a whole shall be submitted for the vote of the Imperial Legislative Council.

11. The term of office of members shall be five years.

12. The matters mentioned hereinbelow shall be exclusively under the control of the Imperial Legislative Council:—

(*a*) Matters in regard to which uniform legislation for the whole of India is desirable.

(*b*) Provincial legislation in so far as it may affect inter-provincial fiscal relations.

(*c*) Questions affecting purely Imperial Revenue, excepting tributes from Indian States.

(*d*) Questions affecting purely Imperial expenditure, except that no resolution of the Imperial Legislative Council shall be binding the Governor-General in Council in respect of military charges for the defence of the country.

(*e*) The right of revising Indian tariffs and customs-duties, of imposing, altering, or removing any tax or cess, modifying the existing system of currency and banking, and granting any aids or bounties to any or all deserving and nascent industries of the country.

(*f*) Resolutions on all matters relating to the administration of the country as a whole.

13. A Resolution passed by the Legislative Council should be binding on the Executive Government, unless vetoed by the Governor-General in Council: provided however that if the resolution is again passed by the Council after an interval of not less than one year, it must be given effect to.

14. A motion for adjournment may be brought forward for the discussion of a definite matter of urgent public importance, if supported by not less than one-eighth of the members present.

15. When the Crown chooses to exercise its power of veto in regard to a Bill passed by a Provincial Legislative Council or by the Imperial Legislative Council, it should be exercised within twelve months from the date on which it is passed, and the Bill shall cease to have effect as from the date on which the fact of such veto is made known to the Legislative Council concerned.

16. The Imperial Legislative Council shall have no power to interfere with the Gover ment of India's direction of the military affairs and the foreign and political relations of India, including the declaration of war, the making of peace and the entering into treaties.

IV.—The Government of India.

1. The Governor-General of India will be the head of the Government of India.

2. He will have an Executive Council, half of whom shall be Indians.

3. The Indian members should be elected by the elected members of the Imperial Legislative Council.

4. Members of the Indian Civil Service shall not ordinarily be appointed to the Executive Council of the Governor-General.

5. The power of making all appointments in the Imperial Civil Services shall vest in the Government of India, as constituted under this scheme, due regard being paid to existing interests, subject to any laws that may be made by the Imperial Legislative Council.

6. The Government of India shall not ordinarily interfere in the local affairs of a province, and powers not specially given to a Provincial Government, shall be deemed to be vested in the former. The authority of the Government of India will ordinarily be limited to general supervision and superintendence over the Provincial Governments.

7. In legislative and administrative matters the Government of India, as constituted under this scheme, shall, as far as possible, be independent of the Secretary of State.

8. A system of independent audit of the accounts of the Government of India should be instituted.

V.—The Secretary of State in Council.

1. The Council of the Secretary of State for India should be abolished.

2. The salary of the Secretary of State should be placed on the British Estimates.

3. The Secretary of State should, as far as possible, occupy the same position in relation to the Government of India, as the Secretary of State for the Colonies does in relation to the Governments of the self-governing Dominions.

4. The Secretary of State for India should be assisted by two Permanent Under-Secretaries, one of whom should always be an Indian.

VI.—India and the Empire.

1. In any Council or other body which may be constituted or convened for the settlement or control of Imperial affairs, India shall be adequately represented in like manner with the Dominions and with equal rights.

2. Indians should be placed on a footing of equality in respect of status and rights of citizenship with other subjects of His Majesty the King throughout the Empire.

VII.—Military and other matters.

Commissions in the Army

1. The military and naval services of His Majesty, both in their commissioned and non-commissioned ranks, should be thrown open to Indians and adequate provision should be made for their selection, training and instruction in India.

Volunteering

2. Indians should be allowed to enlist as volunteers.

Separation of judicial and executive functions

3. Executive Officers in India shall have no judicial powers entrusted to them, and the judiciary in every province shall be placed under the highest Court of that province.

SYED MOHAMMED,
N. SUBBA RAU,
General Secretaries.

APPENDIX III.

A JOINT ADDRESS from Europeans and Indians to His Excellency the Viceroy and Governor-General and the Right Honourable the Secretary of State for India.

THE following is a record of meetings, held at Darjeeling and Calcutta, to discuss the position created by the pronouncement of the 20th of August on Indian Policy, by the Imperial Government:—

"*The policy of His Majesty's Government, with which the Government of India are in complete accord, is that of increasing the association of Indians in every branch of the administration and the gradual development of self-governing institutions with a view to the progressive realization of responsible government in India, as an integral part of the British Empire. They have decided that substantial steps in this direction should be taken as soon as possible, and that it is of the highest importance, as a preliminary to considering what these steps should be, that there should be a free and informal exchange of opinion between those in authority at Home and in India. His Majesty's Government have accordingly decided, with His Majesty's approval, that I should accept the Viceroy's invitation to proceed to India to discuss these matters with the Viceroy and the Government of India, to consider with the Viceroy the views of Local Governments, and to receive the suggestions of representative bodies and others. I would add that progress in this policy can only be achieved by successive stages. The British Government and the Government of India, on whom the responsibility lies for the welfare and advancement of the Indian peoples, must be judges of the time and measure of each advance, and they must be guided by the co-operation received from those upon whom new opportunities of service will thus be conferred and by the extent to which it is found that confidence can be reposed in their sense of responsibility. Ample opportunity will be afforded for the public discussion of the proposals, which will be submitted in due course to Parliament.*"

I.—PRINCIPLES.

The Imperial Government having sent the Secretary of State to India for the purpose of gathering the opinions of all sections, we feel that the members of both the communities should discuss together the advice to be offered to the

Government, bearing in mind that future generations are more affected than ourselves by changes about to be made. We also think that, in times like these, anything of the nature of civil discord amongst those not called upon for active service is out of place. Our opinion is that Europeans and Indians should first agree as to the main outlines which they think the pending reforms should follow. These outlines having been settled, it will then be possible for the different sections to formulate their own views as to details, in respect of which it would be to the public advantage that the Government should have every shade of opinion before them. The agreement relates only to the points printed in black type.

Turning then to the recent pronouncement, we note that it was issued as embodying the policy of the Imperial Government upon which the three principal parties in Great Britain are now represented. As no contrary motion has been raised in either House, it must, in accordance with all precedents, be recognized as a declaration of policy accepted unanimously by the supreme legislature of the British Commonwealth.

In view of these considerations **we agree to accept the pronouncement of the 20th August as common ground, within the limits of which the discussion can take place.**

We have next to consider the positions implied in this pronouncement To begin with we note that for the first time in any official pronouncement the vague and ambiguous term 'self-government' is replaced by the plain and definite words 'responsible government,' which necessarily means the creation of executives responsible to, and therefore removable at the will of, elective bodies and electorates. This principle finds no expression in the various proposals already before the public on the 20th of August, which were all inspired by the looser conception embodied in the words 'self-government.' The pronouncement thus creates a new position, which cannot be met by the adoption of any scheme of reforms as yet submitted for public consideration.

We agree that, having accepted the pronouncement, we are not only free, but even bound to consider the new situation created thereby with open minds.

We are further of opinion that the direction of any steps taken in the immediate future ought to be considered first and foremost from the point of view whether they are calculated to lead towards the goal presented in the pronouncement under review. The necessary criterion, whereby all immediate proposals must be judged, is a clear conception of the ultimate goal, however remote. That goal is defined as 'responsible government in India as an integral part of the British Empire.' This implies the calling into existence in India of a self-governing nation or nations, on the lines of the great self-governing Dominions. The all-important question is, therefore, raised, whether India is to be regarded, like the continent of Europe, as the future home of a number of self-governing nations, or else like the United States as it would have been, had it developed as a British Dominion, a nation living within the bounds of one territory, but in size so great that it must be divided into a number of self-governing provinces. Is India to become a nation or a continent of nations, a Dominion or a group of Dominions? Are the separate provinces to be developed as separate self-governing nations? Or are we to look forward to a time, however remote, when interests common to India will be controlled by a Government responsible to India as a whole?

For those who accept the pronouncement the answer will be found implicit in its terms. Bengal, Madras, Bombay, Bihar and Orissa, the United Provinces and the Punjab are indeed units of population equal or approximating to the scale of great European powers. But, if developed as self-governing nations, their future electorates would still be unable to control railways, tariffs, commercial law, and other major interests common to India as a whole. The control of interests, purely Indian, would still have to be exercised in the future, however distant, by the Imperial Government of the British Commonwealth. Responsible government for India in Indian affairs could never be realized under these conditions. The history of the United Kingdom of Canada, of Australia and of South Africa proves that national self-government cannot be realized here for any unit smaller than the Indian Peninsula. However formidable that enterprise may seem, and however remote its ultimate attainment, that goal must be adopted by those who accept the pronouncement and read its terms in the light of the experience gained in the other Dominions. In the comprehensive nationhood of India, to be called into being in centuries to come; the individualities of the Bengalee, the Maratha, the Sikh, the Canarese and all the other numerous races must each find their place as sub-nationalities, like those of the English, Scotch, Welsh and Irish in the United Kingdom, and like those of the British and French in Canada. The goal to be kept in mind must, therefore, be, not the nations of Europe, but rather the United States as it would have been had it developed as a self-governing dominion of the British Commonwealth. However remote the realization of this conception may be, steps to be taken in the immediate future must yet be judged by the criterion whether they tend towards that goal.

To begin with, we are bound to consider how far the existing map is in harmony with this conception.

The map of India has been designed to suit the needs of a great dependency, whose internal and domestic affairs are subject in every detail to direction from an authority on the other side of the world. A government, whose mainspring is outside the area it is governing, has no difficulty in uniting under one administrative machine, not only communities which are different in character, but separate territories. Under this system, the Imperial Government had no difficulty in incorporating Burma as a province of India. But if India is now to be governed with a view to becoming a self-governing nation, Burma, by reason of her situation, never can have a place in its national fabric. She has less in common with India than Ceylon. Her affinities with India are less than those of Finland with Russia, or of Mexico with the United States. The project of developing India as a self-governing nation can be rendered less formidable at once by eliminating Burma. It has no place in the picture. It ought to be put in the same category as Ceylon, and nothing in these suggestions should be taken as referring to Burma.

In like manner, the conception, abandoned in the recent pronouncement, has operated to divide India into a few great satrapies commensurate with the principal nations of Europe. In Bombay, it has united communities so diverse as Sind, the Marathas and the Canarese. No less artificial is the union of Bihar with Orissa. In the United Provinces more than 48,000,000 souls have been brought under the rule of a single officer, and so long as these Governments are solely amenable to a Government which takes its direction from London, no difficulty is experienced. But the moment any real beginning in responsible government is made, and executives responsible to electorates are created, however limited the powers entrusted to them may be to begin with, such combinations will surely break down. They will fail as certainly as did the attempt to unite Ontario and Quebec under one executive reponsible to a common electorate. The foundations of Canadian nationhood were only laid by according separate provincial governments to both the races, under which each race could enjoy unhampered its own language, religion and system of law. The examples of the United States, Canada, Australia and South Africa, as contrasted with India, China and the dependencies of Spain and France in the eighteenth century, prove that under elective institutions provincial administration cannot be made effective for units of population the size of great nations. Had the United States attempted to develop herself on the basis of five or six provinces, each would, for administrative reasons, have been driven to subdivide itself into minor self-governing provinces commensurate in size with the existing forty-eight States. County Councils or District Boards cannot take the place of Provincial Governments, which in nations of a certain magnitude, must be interposed between local authorities on the one hand, and the national Government on the other. Hence, the Government of the United Kingdom with its population of 45,000,000 is increasingly unable to cope with their need for social reform.

Thus, had America tried to develop on the basis of five or six provinces, each with subordinate provinces, each therefore on the scale, and organized on the pattern, of great federal nations, each would have felt and acted as nations. They would have fallen apart, and the United States would have failed to achieve national unity in accordance with the demands of nature and good government. Her territory would have become the home of five or six nations, with no common control of interests common to all. Like Europe or South America, she would have become the theatre of ceaseless wars, instead of the home of internal peace.

The conclusion is that it is impossible for India to develop as a self-governing Dominion or to achieve a genuine nationhood in the future, however distant, on the basis of a map inherited from the Môghul Empire and fashioned to suit the needs of an administration which has its mainspring in England. We agree, therefore, that the selection of areas capable of development as the self-governing provinces of a future United States of India within the British Empire should be undertaken at the outset. These areas should be termed "Provincial States" as a reminder that they are designed to serve as the autonomous provinces of the future United States of India within the Empire. The term also recalls the

Native States. Their areas should be commensurate with the larger of those States like Hyderabad and Mysore, and should be determined, so far as possible with reference to history, to community of race, language and religion, and above all to effective self-government on true provincial lines. Care should also be taken not to combine under one Provincial Government areas of totally different types, the economic interests of which are wholly distinct.

So long as an autocratic regime exists, its subdivisions can be re-adjusted with relative ease. But the moment they are made the areas of elective authorities, the difficulty of changing them tends to become insuperable. Had the States of America been too large at the outset to serve as the ultimate areas of provincial autonomy, no power could alter them now, short of conquest or civil war. The Kingdom of Prussia overshadows all Germany, and no one dares to suggest its partition into provinces commensurate with its partners. To-day it needs but the nerve and foresight of a statesman to find and fix areas in India capable of developing into effective self-governing provinces, and yet such as will admit of her growth as a nation at unity with herself.

We agree, therefore, that the existing provinces need not be assumed to be areas suitable as a basis for responsible government, but such areas must be settled at the moment when the first instalment of responsible government is granted.

Bearing in mind, then, the picture of India as a self-governing Dominion of the federal type, we recognize that, in the words of the pronouncement before us, 'progress in this policy can only be achieved by successive stages.' There must be stages, and the questions before us are, where those stages should begin, and what they should be. Reason and experience alike point to the conclusion that it is not in the sphere of the central Government that the beginning should be made. Whether in the case of the United States of America, of Canada, Australia or South Africa, nothing was done, or could have been done, to create a central and national Government responsible to the nation as a whole, until responsible government had been completely and finally established in the several provinces. This does not imply that changes cannot, or ought not, to be made whereby public opinion may be voiced more freely in the counsels of the central authority, while that authority remains in theory and practice responsible to the Secretary of State. But responsible government means entrusting some functions to executives which hold office, and can be dismissed from office, by elected legislatures or electorates. That principle must first be tried and established in the provinces. It is only when provincial executives are answerable for all their functions to provincial electorates that the Indian executive can be rendered answerable to, and removable by, an Indian Parliament and an Indian Electorate.

We, therefore, agree that the first steps towards responsible government cannot be taken in the sphere of the central Government.

We have next to consider the fact that administrative mechanism designed to obey an authority remote from India itself cannot, as it stands, respond to the impetus of Indian electorates. Mechanism must be adapted to the nature of the force which drives it. The whole administrative system of England would have to be revised, if the control of the electorate were replaced by a centralized power exercised from without. The reverse is equally true of India. If electorates are to be given responsibilities however limited, they must to a great extent, and to an increasing degree, operate through departments, organized on principles different from those of the present machinery. With the introduction of responsible government it is necessary, therefore, to contemplate a change, not only of areas, but also in the character of the departments through which the electorates are to operate. The existing provincial administrations cannot be moulded by a series of gradual changes into the provinces of a self-governing Dominion. Their place must gradually be taken by provincial organs of a new type. The first step must be to create new organs responsible to the electorates of suitable areas. To these, specified functions, together with corresponding revenues and powers and additional taxation, must be transferred. All other functions must be reserved to the existing provincial Governments, to be transferred by successive stages to the elective organs, as each may prove its capacity for assuming the additional burden.

It follows, therefore, that during the period of transition governments of two different types will have to exist side by side. No instalment of responsible government can be granted without creating executives responsible to, and therefore removable by, elective assemblies and electorates for certain functions and revenues within suitable areas. Meanwhile, the powers not yet transferred must be exercised by the existing provincial Governments, which must be kept in being for that purpose, and remain responsible to, and therefore removable only by, the Government of India, the Secretary of State and finally Parliament itself. If responsible government is the goal, the only other alternative is sooner or later to transfer all powers of government at one stroke to executives removable at the will of Indian electorates. But this course is expressly barred by the terms of the pronouncement we have agreed to accept. It follows that in the transition stage governments of two different types must co-exist, the one responsible to electorates, the other to the Secretary of State. In our opinion, therefore, it is of the utmost importance to insist now that the responsibility must in either case be a real one. The responsibility of the new executives to their assemblies and electorates, however limited their functions, must be real. It must not be confused and destroyed by a net-work of minor restrictions and sanctions. On the other hand, the responsibility of the old governments to the Secretary of State for the functions reserved to them must be no less a real one. In discharging those functions, they can and should be exposed in every detail to the criticism and influence of Indian opinion. But in the last analysis the ultimate power of decision in respect of those functions must be reserved to the Secretary of State and his agents, until they can be transferred to the executives responsible to the electorates. And, in the words of the pronouncement, 'the British Government and the Government of India must be judges of the time and measure of each advance.'

We agree, therefore, that, during the period of transition, Governments of two types must co-exist, the one responsible to electorates for specific powers, the other to the Secretary of State for all other powers, and that the responsibility of each must in fact be a real one, and their powers must be sufficient to enable them to discharge that responsibility efficiently.

We have now to approach the question how new organs of provincial government responsible to electorates can be brought into being. The first preliminary is to create these electorates, and also to provide an adequate supply of leaders competent to guide them and to translate their mandates into action and law.

With a view to providing men in some sort competent to act as members of popular legislatures and executives, there are improvements which might be made in the existing system. Executive Councils might be introduced in the

United Provinces, the Punjab and the Central Provinces, and Indians, not exceeding in number half the members other than the head of the province, might be appointed to each. A second Indian Member might be added to the Executive Councils already in being. But these suggestions, if adopted, would add but half a dozen to the number of Indians in touch with administrative detail; of greater importance therefore is the suggestion that the unofficial Members of Provincial Councils should be divided into committees, severally attached to the Members of Council, in much the same relation as the India Council is attached to the Secretary of State. In this capacity they would see and advise upon cases submitted to their opinion by their Member of Council, and thus gain an insight into administrative conditions. The most valuable of these changes can be made without legislation and might, therefore, be effected as quickly as possible. They will help to prepare legislators and ministers for the first experiments in responsible government.

On the other hand, they will do nothing to prepare electorates. Electoral figures have never been published; but in parts of Northern India they are known scarcely to exceed one twothousandth part of the population. But electorates of an adequate strength and quality are the necessary foundation of responsible government. There must be an adequate number of citizens to whom Government is answerable, and from whom, therefore, Government can derive its authority; and those citizens must be capable in some sort of understanding the questions submitted to their judgment, of placing the public interest before their own, of doing justice to each other, and, what is of even greater importance, to those outside the electorate, even at the sacrifice of their personal interests. The material for such electorates is sadly deficient, and must be created. To argue that this can be done merely by extending the type of education given in schools and colleges is a dangerous fallacy. On the contrary, as all experience shows, a general extension of education without a simultaneons extension of political responsibility ends by sapping the foundations of government. A great improvement and extension of education throughout India is urgently needed. But wisdom can only be learned from the teaching of experience itself, and all that education can do is to open a people's mind, and enable them to read the lessons of experience which the exercise of responsibility alone can bring.

In order to train voters for the task of government, some responsibilities for government must be laid upon them. Until this is done, the process of political education has not been started. The gradual extension of such responsibilities must go side by side with the extension of education. Nor do we consider that this can now be limited with safety to the sphere of Local Government, which, of necessity, deals with administrative details only. The time is at hand when some responsibility for considering and deciding questions of principle, some political responsibility, that is to say, ought to be placed on the shoulders of electorates. Thus, while we do not think it is possible at this stage to make such changes in the Government of India, we think that the time has past when the principle of responsible government can be limited, as it now is, to the sphere of local administration. If genuine electorates are to be called into being, some responsibilities of a provincial nature must first be laid upon them, and afterwards increased, as the electorates can be strengthened and enlarged, and can demonstrate capacity for bearing the burden. To make that burden too heavy at the outset is to jeopardise the whole project. No prudent person, for instance, would suggest that they should be made responsible for the maintenance of law and order to begin with. To do so, would be risking a break-down, which more than anything would delay progress towards complete responsible government. To begin with, the old experienced Government must stand by to maintain order, and discharge those functions upon which the immediate stability of the social fabric depends. The first powers to be transferred to electorates should be those connected with social reforms, with the future building up of society, like education and Local Government. As soon as electorates have proved themselves capable of discharging these functions, it will be time to transfer others, the neglect of which is more quickly felt. We think, as a general proposition, that an electorate may be deemed fit for the exercise of full responsible government whenever it has been entrusted with, and has proved its competence in the control of, Police and Justice.

In our opinion, therefore, a beginning should be made in training electorates by making them responsible for certain provincial functions. But the training will not be effective, unless the system is so simplified that electors can easily trace the effect of the votes they cast. The existing tangled and complicated system of election is destructive of all educational result so far as political responsibility is concerned. The ordinary voter cannot possibly foresee the result of his vote on the Provincial Council, still less on the Imperial body. Besides which the existing system is an incentive to corruption. If only to render corruption more difficult, the initial electorates should be as large as possible. They should include those whose pockets will be directly affected by the votes they cast, for it is thus that the connection of cause and effect is first brought home to electors.

Above all, the method of voting must be direct. Indirect election not only destroys the educational value of the system, but destroys responsibility itself. It is really a device for concealing the fact that adequate electorates do not exist and evades the difficult truth that they cannot be made a reality without giving some responsibilities to some electorates not yet ripe for them and taking inevitable risks.

II.—Outline of the Scheme proposed.

We now propose to outline a scheme of development such as we think would give effect to the principles upon which we have agreed. Having done so, we shall be in a position to suggest the special safeguards which should be accorded to Industrial and Commercial interests. We recognize that the scheme must be one capable of adaptation to suit the highly various conditions and levels of advancement in the different provinces of India. We shall, therefore, sketch the scheme as we think it might be applied to a particular province, taking as our example one, which is not so advanced as the old Presidencies, but perhaps more so than other parts of India. For this purpose we select the United Provinces, which has the advantage of being, not only central, but also the largest in India.

In this Province we suggest the old Kingdom of Oudh as an area suitable to form a Provincial State in the future self-governing Dominion. Another might be formed from the divisions surrounding Benares, a third from the Doab; while those to the North-West might be grouped round Meerut. Primitive communities, like those of the hill districts of Kumaon and Bundelkhand and of Mirzapur, might, to begin with, be reserved to the present Government of the United Provinces. This Government, subject to certain changes, which we shall outline later, would remain in being, holding and exercising all powers which had not been transferred to the four Provincial States.

The first step would be to create the largest electorates which may be deemed possible under existing conditions, in accordance with the principles suggested above. Indian conditions are so various that these principles must be applied in harmony with the conditions of each Provincial State.

These electorates should elect assemblies consisting of from 45 to 75 members each. To these bodies should be transferred at least the present functions of the District Boards, coupled with the control now exercised by the Government over those functions. In order to simplify the electoral system, as far as possible at the outset, and avoid confusing the minds of inexperienced voters by numerous elections, those of the District Boards might be abolished for the present in backward provinces at any rate. The Boards might be appointed by the Government of the Provincial State until it sees fit to re-establish an electoral system for the districts.

The municipalities would, of course, remain as at present, but would be transferred to the control of the Provincial State. The creation of panchayats and other local authorities would also be included within its legislative powers.

By this scheme the new Governments would at once be vested with the full control throughout their areas of—

Roads and Bridges. | Primary Education.
Local Government.

To these in the United Provinces we think that Agriculture, and in Bengal that higher education, should be added.

The administration of these functions would rest with a Ministry drawn from the assembly and responsible thereto. The Ministry would consist of five portfolios :—

A Minister of Public Works.
Ditto of Education.
Ditto of Local Government.
Ditto of Agriculture.
Ditto of Finance.

The Ministry would be called into being as follows. An officer, presumably the senior commissioner in each Provincial State, would be made the superior officer of the other Commissioner or Commissioners in that area. As Chief Commissioner he would thus control all the officers in charge of the reserved functions retained by the Government of the United Provinces. He would also act as the constitutional head of the Provincial State, that is to say in the capacity of the

Governor of a Province like Quebec or Tasmania. In that capacity he would send for the Member of the newly elected assembly who, in his judgment, was best qualified to command the support of that body, and would ask him to form a Ministry.

The Ministry, when formed, would then proceed to design departmental machinery suitable for administering the various functions under their portfolios. Their new departments would be staffed from officers taken over from the services of the United Provinces, all existing rights of officers being strictly safeguarded by law. In this operation they would be assisted, not only by the Chief Commissioner, but also by a Civil Service Commission of three, with reference to which we have more to say hereafter. Ministers would not be expected to take over their functions from the old Government until the arrangements for the necessary departments were complete.

The relations of the Chief Commissioner to his Ministers are of great importance. An undivided responsibility would rest on Ministers, so far as the functions transferred to them are concerned. They would be responsible to the assembly for their decisions, and, provided they were *intra vires*, the Chief Commissioner would have to give legal effect to those decisions by his signature. No responsibility would rest upon him in respect of the transferred powers. But before signing their decisions he would have every opportunity of giving his Ministers advice, and, if they were wise, they would avail themselves of his advice to the full. They would do so the more readily in that an undivided control of their own functions would rest with themselves. They would be responsible to the assembly, and the assembly to the electorate; and a chain of responsibility at once simple and clear, between the elector and the administrative officer, would thus be established.

The Chief Commissioner would thus be in a position to guide his Ministers in the execution of the transferred powers by his influence and advice. On the other hand, he would control all the officers of the United Provinces in charge of the reserved functions within the area of the Provincial State. He would thus be well situated to smooth away the causes of friction inevitable between the two authorities. In all federal systems at least two authorities must administer their different functions within the same area, and some friction always exists. Whether the system works or not, simply depends upon the efficacy of the means provided for reducing the friction and of disposing of questions at issue between the two organs of Government.

We agree that a share of the consolidated revenue of the Province should be handed over to the Provincial State Governments, proportionate to the cost of the functions transferred to them; in addition to which should be handed over certain specific powers of taxation, such as would fall on the Provincial State electorate itself.

This is essential to any genuine scheme of responsible government. The electors must learn from experience that, if they demand an extension of services placed under their control, the cost of the extension must also be met from their own resources. This condition is vital to their political training. The taxes imposed by them can still be collected by the existing Board of Revenue, as happens at present with the cesses imposed by District Boards. The taxes, however, imposed by the Provincial State Government should be collected from the tax-payer on separate and distinctive notes of demand so that he may clearly recognize that the charge is one imposed by his own representatives.

The finances of the Provincial States should be subject to the same audit as those of the United Provinces itself, that is to say of the Finance Department of the Government of India. The auditors should disallow any expenditure outside the powers of the Provincial State, and institute enquiries, when any trace of corruption is found. They should also disallow all unauthorized expenditure, but on this, and, generally, on all matters relating to financial administration, they should report direct to the Committee of Public Accounts of the State assembly.

The Government of the United Provinces might be empowered to make grants-in-aid of certain objects, subject to inspection, the payments to depend upon the Provincial State Government having carried out those objects to the satisfaction of the Inspectors. But otherwise checks and sanctions in detail should be studiously avoided, for two reasons. In the first place, they are the most fertile cause of friction. In the second place, they undermine the responsibility which ought to rest on the new Governments and their electorates. The Government of the Province will, of course, retain the usual power of veto over legislation passed by Provincial State assemblies; and borrowing would be subject to Government control.

Otherwise, we believe, that the one sound and effective check will be found in a power of total suspension held in reserve. If the Government of a Provincial State prove its utter incompetence, the assembly should be dissolved, and the issue referred to the electors. If then the electors fail to establish a Government competent to put matters straight, and their area remains a scene of neglect, corruption or disorder, the system must be suspended for that area. The Provincial Government will be there to resume their functions and to set the Provincial State in order, just as is done in the case of Native States, continuing to administer until the time seems ripe for a fresh beginning of responsible government In the case of civil disorders, brought about by the intolerance of a Provincial State Government, there must be powers of summary suspension. We return to this subject also later.

The initial experiment would be started for a definite period of, say, seven years. At the end of that period the whole system throughout India would be reviewed by a Commission reporting direct to the Secretary of State. The Commission should include men who had served as Governors of Crown and self-governing Colonies. After examining the conditions of each Provincial State on the spot, the Commissioners would report whether fresh powers should be granted such as the control of irrigation and forests, of higher education, of local railways, of famine relief, and so forth. Or it might report that the Government had done so indifferently that the existing powers should merely be renewed. Lastly, in cases of total failure, it should have powers to report in favour of suspension ; but, before the Secretary of State takes final action, the papers should be laid before both Houses of Parliament.

It must, at the outset, be laid down that during the seven years' period no claim can be entertained for further administrative powers or a further share of the consolidated revenue of the province. This is essential in the interests of the new electoral bodies themselves. Their whole energies must be reserved for the task of justifying the powers already assigned to them and thus establishing their claim to further powers at the end of the period. If the attention of the electorates is continuously diverted from social reforms to agitation for political change, progress towards responsible government is foredoomed from the outset. The dates at which claims for further changes are to be considered should be fixed in advance, and the machinery whereby those claims are to be decided on the basis of fact and experience should be settled from the outset.

We agree that in the intervening periods no demand for further executive powers or for a further share of existing revenues should be entertained.

This does not apply, however, to legislative powers. Again we are keeping in mind the picture of India, as she will be when constitutional finality is attained, and all matters, domestic to India, are subject either to her Provincial State assemblies, or to an Indian Parliament. In the work of framing the final constitution, the task of apportioning the legislative powers between the National Government on the one hand and those of the Provincial States on the other, will be difficult indeed, unless, during the period of transition, the problem has been worked out and solved by the test of experience. To this end we suggest that Provincial State assemblies shall be encouraged to petition the Provincial Governments, from time to time, for legislative powers they desire to exercise. The petition would be cast into the form of an enabling Bill submitted to the Legislative Council of the Province. The Bill, after first and second reading, would be referred to a committee upon which the Provincial Government would appoint a majority of members. The procedure of the committee would be exactly that of a Standing Committee of Parliament appointed to deal with Bills promoted by local authorities. Counsel would be heard on behalf of the promoters, and of all interests affected by the Bill. The preamble would have to be proved. The clauses would then be considered, passed, negatived or amended; and evidence for or against the contentions of those promoting the Bill would be heard. The enabling Bill, if passed into an Act, would then define with accuracy the limits within which the Provincial State assembly could legislate on the subject.

The same method is applicable to new sources of revenue. A Provincial State Government might desire to increase its revenues by a stamp on patent medicines sold within its area. It would then be open to it to embody the proposal in an enabling Bill, and to bring it before the Legislative Council of the Province. Under the Bill, if passed, its assembly would then pass legislation imposing the new tax. Thus by means of experiment, appropriate sources of Provincial State revenue would be discovered.

At the close of each period of seven years, the Commissioners would review the results, and advise whether the powers so obtained by one Provincial State should be extended to all. The Government of India should be free, at any moment, to generalize such powers by legislation. In this way, whenever the time comes to create a government for India responsible to an Indian electorate, the legislative powers appropriate to the Provincial States will have been ascertained by the only trustworthy tests, those of trial and experience.

That time will have arrived whenever a sufficient number of Provincial States have acquired the control of justice, jails and police and have proved their competence for the fundamental task of Government, that of maintaining order. The confirmation of a Provincial State in those powers will amount to a final certificate of the fitness of its electorate for full responsible government. When a sufficient number of Provincial State electorates have acquired that certificate, the time will have come to summon their representatives to a National Convention to devise a constitution, under which the Government of India can be made responsible to an Indian Parliament and electorate; and the constitution, like those framed by the representatives of the Canadian, Australian and South African Provinces, will acquire legal effect as a statute of the Imperial Parliament. In matters common to all India, responsible government cannot be introduced by stages. It must be introduced at one stroke, by one instrument of Government—the constitution of India, under which she will assume her final place in the Commonwealth of Nations. That can only take place when a sufficient number of Provincial States have established and proved their competence for responsible government. The stones will then have been quarried and shaped from which the final edifice can be built.

The old Provincial Governments will, of course, vanish the moment their final powers have passed to their Provincial States. But the question of reforms, such as will fit them to fulfil their transitional functions, is of great importance. Their functions will be to hold and administer the reserved powers until the last final function, that of maintaining order, can be handed over. But another and even more important function will be that of supervising the acquisition by the Provincial States of new legislative powers and sources of revenue, which, of course, they will do subject to the direction of the Government of India.

As stated already, we assume that Executive Councils will be established in all but the minor provinces, one half of which will be Indian; a majority being retained for the European members by the Governor's casting vote.

The Legislative Councils should be composed mainly of delegations from the assemblies of the Provincial States, together with some additional members appointed by Government to represent special interests. There is nothing to prevent the introduction of officials at any time who are required to discuss matters within their expert knowledge. But official voters should vanish. The existing system of official members voting by order, irrespective of their personal views, is derogatory to their own position, wasteful of their valuable time, fatal to principles which should govern public debate, and eminently calculated to create a feeling of antagonism between Indians and Europeans as such. It is also insincere. If Government cannot accept a motion of whatever kind, let the Governor say so, and let that suffice. A final difference of opinion between the Government responsible to the Secretary of State and the spokesmen of public opinion is not mended by the practice of annulling the votes of elected members by those of officials' cast, under orders of Government. Let the Councils consist entirely of non-official members, the members of the Executive Council and such other officials as they choose to bring with them appearing only for the purposes of debate. Let every detail of administration, of legislation and of the estimates be brought before the Council for discussion. Let the work of Government be exposed to unofficial criticism and influence from end to end. The onus of final decision in matters for which the executives are responsible to the Government of India and to the Secretary of State rests with them, subject, of course, to the provision that those superior authorities can always reverse the decision of their agents, on petition from the Legislative Councils. Just as the responsibility of the Provincial State ministers to their assemblies and electorates must be unhampered and clear, so also must be that of the Provincial executives to the Government of India and the Secretary of State.

That the two principles are inseparable will be seen by reference to the procedure whereby the Legislative Councils will deal with enabling Bills promoted by Governments of Provincial States. The Legislative Councils will mainly consist of delegations from those bodies, one of which is promoting the

Bill. An assembly so formed will be likely to voice every kind of opinion which may be held with regard to the new legislative powers sought therein. On second reading, on report stage and on third reading its members will have every opportunity of doing so. The assembly will send members to the Select Committee. Government will thus have access to every phase of public opinion on the subject, as well as to the views of the Government of India, which will hold a brief for the future federal Government of India. But clearly the power of final decision on any disputed point could not be left with the spokesmen of the Provincial State assemblies. The system will not work, unless the responsibility of either authority for the functions assigned it is real; which cannot be, unless its power is equivalent to its responsibility. The most important of all the responsibilities reserved to the old Governments in the transitional stage is that 'of judging of the time and measure of each advance.'

We consider that the Imperial Legislative Council should be reformed on the same principles. The official votes should vanish and the members should be largely recruited by proportional representation from the Provincial State assemblies and other public bodies as at present.

As the transfer of officers is likely to prove more delicate and difficult than the transfer of powers, the subject has been left for separate treatment. Our view is that there should be attached to the Government of India and to the Government of each province a standing commission of three senior officers, one of whom should always be an Indian. These Commissioners should inspect and be cognizant of the work of every department, and of every officer in those departments. It should be their duty to bring to the notice of Government all cases of over or under employment, of overlapping and of all defects in organization. They would serve in fact as the Consulting Engineers of the administrative machine. They would have no powers but those of report. It would rest with Governments to give effect to their recommendations. A vast human machine, which is always being changed and increased, requires continuous inspection of experts who stand outside it and view it as a whole. Government which is part of the mechanism has no time to do this; and, without the advice of such experts, the gradual adjustments required to keep it in gear, and to avoid overlapping and waste, are not perceived and made in time. When the whole structure has grown thoroughly obsolete and clearly unsuited to public needs, a Civil Service Commission is appointed, largely consisting of amateurs. An elaborate enquiry is undertaken at vast expense. Questions are put which are difficult for officials to answer with honesty in public A great strain is put on their time and a great disturbance of the public mind is occasioned. Their recommendations involve changes so great that it is very difficult to carry them into effect, whereas those changes, if effected gradually, as the need had arisen, could easily have been made.

This is one aspect of the permanent Civil Service Commissions which exist in the Dominions. But there is another and even more important feature of the institution as it exists in Australia and New Zealand. Appointments and promotions are, of course, made by the Government, but on the advice of the Commissioners. Government is not bound to take their advice, but if it departs therefrom, it is bound to record its reasons for the information of the legislature. The plan has been devised to relieve Government of the demoralising burden of patronage, which consumes the time and energy of its members urgently needed for administrative work. In effecting this object, the permanent Advisory Commission has proved successful.

In India, we think that all appointments should be made on the advice of such Commissioners. Three should be attached to the Government of India, and three to each of the provinces. Where the Government of India or Provincial Governments depart from their advice, their reasons should be recorded for the information of the Secretary of State; where Provincial State ministers are unable to take their advice, their reasons should be recorded and submitted to their Legislative assemblies.

The Standing Commissions would play an important part in the transfer of officers to the departments of the new elective authorities. Such transfers would be voluntary so far as is possible. Ministers, with the advice and assistance of the Chief Commissioner, would arrange for the voluntary transfer of officers from the old departments to their own. But where voluntary arrangements failed, the transfer would be effected on the advice of the Commissioners, to which effect would be given by the Provincial Government, subject to the conditions specified above. The organization of the new departments would also proceed subject to the expert advice of the Commissioners.

III.—Safeguards.

We have outlined a scheme such as we think is capable of being adapted to varying conditions in the different provinces of British India. But wherever, as in Bengal, there exist commercial and industrial interests representing great investments of capital, we consider that special safeguards are necessary, less in the interests of the investors than of the people of India themselves. Responsible government cannot be initiated or advanced without an increase of public expenditure. A development of natural resources is essential in order to provide the additional revenue. But development requires a free investment of capital from without, and nothing could be more fatal to the prospects of such investment than to allow an impression, however unfounded, to take root at this juncture that existing investments of capital are not secure. Unless special safeguards are provided at the outset, fears will exist in the money markets of the world that existing interests may be subject to injury, either by reason of predatory or regulative legislation, or by reason of neglect of transportation and other facilities. It is wise to allay these fears at the outset.

In the first place, all legislation will be subject to the veto of the Indian and Provincial Governments subject to the Secretary of State. In Dominion constitutions, the Acts of Parliament, embodying the powers of the Dominion Governments, do not include most important constitutional provisions, those governing the relations of the Dominion to the Imperial Government. Such provisions will be found in the instructions issued to the Governors by the Imperial Government.

It is in instructions issued by the Imperial Government to the Government of India, that securities against legislation injurious to commercial and industrial interests can be given. In these instructions it should be laid down that legislation affecting commercial and industrial undertakings should be reserved for the sanction of the Secretary of State, and a limit of time should be laid down, within which representatives from the interests affected can be received by him.

We agree that instructions to this effect should be included in a schedule attached to the Act of Parliament in which the scheme of reforms is embodied.

This will not, however, allay the fears of those who have invested their capital in plantations and other industrial undertakings scattered about the country, lest the value of their property may be ruined by neglect of transportation facilities, of protection from flood, water-supply and of other public utilities.

Where damage to industrial interests from such neglect can be proved, the Provincial Government should have power to step in, and do the necessary work at the cost of the Provincial State Government in default. Throughout the period of transition the Provincial Government responsible to the Secretary of State will be in existence and in a position to provide the necessary remedy. That Government will vanish only when the Provincial State Governments within its jurisdiction have finally proved their capacity for efficient administration. The final certificate of efficiency would not be given to a Provincial State Government, so long as it shewed a tendency to neglect public utilities upon which the value of capital invested on productive undertakings in their area depends.

We agree that the Provincial Governments responsible to the Government of India and the Secretary of State shall have power to do or repair public works, upon which the value of invested capital depends, neglect of which is due to the default of Provincial State Governments, and to charge the cost thereof to the revenues assigned to the Government in default.

In this connection we return to the final remedy of recalling powers and of total suspension. It is, however, mainly with a view to the progress of responsible government itself, that we urge that these safeguards should be made real. If India is to move as quickly as possible towards the goal of complete responsible government, each part of India must, in the stage of transition, be enabled to move at its own pace. Government must be ready to reward proof of efficiency in administering powers already granted by a generous transfer of fresh powers. The whole system rests on the principle of placing responsible governments on trial, testing capacity, and making recorded experience the ground of future advance. Such advances should be bold; but advances will not be bold, unless it is understood from the outset that, where steps in advance have clearly been premature, they can be retraced. Experiment is the only sound basis of policy; but no experiment is real, unless Government is able to abide by negative as well as by positive results. Government will make experiments freely, only if it knows that it can and must give practical effect to lessons of failure as well as to those of success. If the right of recall be established, Government should be bold in adding to the powers of progessive electoral authorities. For the rapid advance towards full responsible government of some Provincial States will certainly react on their backward neighbours. Nothing is more contagious than example, and it is to the forward States that we look to set the pace of progress. It should, therefore, be made as safe and easy as possible for Government at stated intervals to add to the powers.

For similar reasons the power of total suspension held in reserve is important. The existence of the power, in fact as well as in law, will largely operate to render its use unnecessary. If the Imperial veto on Colonial legislation is rarely exercised, it is largely because the power, unlike that of the Sovereign, is a real one. Colonial ministers refuse to accept amendments from their own supporters when they know that such amendments, if incorporated in a measure before the legislature, would oblige the Imperial Government to veto it.

In like manner the public disgrace, inseparable from suspension, will act as a spur to the ministers, assemblies and electorates of backward Provincial States, and prevent their allowing the standard of government from degenerating to the point when total suspension is obviously needed in the public interest. Neglect and corruption cannot continue to flourish unchecked in one Provincial State without reacting on the progress of the others. Positive anarchy is infectious and spreads to its neighbours. Just as a progressive State will stimulate progress in those behind it, so a total failure will impede the progress of those in advance of it. The best hope for such a community is the total suspension of its incapable regime as in the case of a Native State where anarchy is rampant. Corruption must be weeded out, injustice must be redressed, public utilities must be restored, and a clean and efficient standard of government re-established, before the community is allowed to begin once more an attempt to do these things for itself. It is on the same principle that in the United Kingdom a constituency, provenly corrupt, is disenfranchised for a period of years.

We agree that the Government of India must have the right to recall powers which have been abused or neglected, and, in extreme cases, to suspend the Governments of Provincial States. Such powers shall always be subject to the sanction of the Secretary of State and of Parliament; but in cases of emergency the Government of India may exercise the power, subject to the subsequent sanction of the Secretary of State and of Parliament.

Lastly, it is necessary to consider how an adequate representation can be secured for those in charge of commercial and industrial undertakings. These are largely financed from capital outside India, and are mainly administered by Europeans. They are in number a mere handful, but, in the interests of the new elective authorities, it is essential that they should be represented in some proportion to the magnitude of the interests they control. It would be a calamity to India if they drifted into the position of Uitlanders Their assistance is needed in building up the fabric of responsibe government. Provincial State ministries and assemblies will have everything to gain by an adequate infusion of a race to whom the working of responsible government is familiar.

We agree that, (a) wherever industrial and commercial interests are located, an adequate representation should be accorded; (b) adequate representation should be accorded to Mahomedans, Land-holders and minorities generally.

IV.—Procedure to be followed in giving effect to the scheme.

The question will naturally be raised how effect can be given to the provisions set out at the end of the last section. The same question arises with regard to a number of other provisions recommended in this note. Any scheme, which suggests at this juncture how India can start on her progress towards responsible government, is open to the same criticism. The new pronouncement was only made on the 20th of August last, and the Secretary of State has reached India within three months from that date. It is utterly beyond the power, even of skilled and experienced officials, to collect within that time the facts and figures necessary before the details of proposals can be worked out. Nor, we venture to predict, will the Secretary of State himself be able to do this, with all the assistance which the Government of India can give him. The short time at his disposal here will be more than occupied with the study of principles, and if any attempt is afterwards made to work these principles into a complete scheme in London, we believe that it will fail for lack of detailed information, which can only be obtained on the spot. Such failure will mean delay, and delay will not be understood in India. It will surely breed distrust and continued agitation. The greatest need of India is that prompt and unmistakable steps should be taken to give effect to the policy outlined in the recent pronouncements. The only way in which this can be done, is by the early enactment of a measure by Parliament such as will set in train the progress of India towards responsible government there foreshadowed.

The solution of the problem, we suggest, will be found in the precedent set by the Government of London Act of 1899. By this measure it was proposed to abolish more than forty vestries, and establish in their place a far smaller number of municipal bodies. The whole scheme, including the constitution of the new bodies, was firmly outlined in the measure. Yet the Parliamentary draughtsman, situated as he was in the middle of the subject dealt with by the measure, with all the forces of the Local Government Board, the Home Office, the London County Council, the City of London, and the Vestries at his disposal, was unable to cope with the innumerable details which had to be worked out before effect could be given to its provisions. In order to bring the new bodies into existence, it was necessary to delimit areas, fix the number of members on the various bodies, adjust their finances, and disentangle and re-arrange a multitude of details. All this was remitted to three Commissioners named and appointed under the Act. The moment the Act was passed the Commissioners got to work, and, as their arrangements were framed, legal effect was given to them by orders in Council issued in terms of its provisions.

We believe that the adoption of this course is the only way to avoid a delay which will prove mischievous in the extreme to the peace and interests of India. It is not delay in bringing into being the new organs of Government that we fear. That of necessity is a task the details of which need time for their execution. Any attempt to burke those details will only end in further postponement. The delay, we fear, is in framing a measure which the Imperial Government can adopt for submission to Parliament, and in the passage of that measure into law. The trust of India in Parliament is unimpaired, and if once the scheme of reforms is firmly outlined in statutory form, and Commissioners are appointed to give effect to it, the people of India will not be found wanting in patience. Their energies will, we think, be devoted to aiding the Government and Commissioners in working out the details and carrying them into effect.

We agree, therefore, in advising that the specific points to which our agreement relates and the outlines of the scheme sketched in these proposals be laid down in an Act of Parliament: but that all questions, within those outlines

relating to franchises, constitutions, powers, finances and such like details be remitted to not more than five Commissioners named under the Act, to be dealt with in India by the Commissioners, in consultation with Governments and People, the arrangements of the Commissioners, to be given the force of law by Orders in Council.

The goal of responsible government having now been declared, the scheme should, in our opinion, be one which initiates not only the immediate steps, but renders visible to the people of India the whole path to the ultimate goal. We urge that the measures should be such as will leave no room for constitutional agitation, either now, or at any future time. It should set them free to devote their whole strength to social and political reform, by placing political as well as social reform within their reach. The situation we desire is one in which communities in all parts of British India can attain to new political powers, always, but only, by proving their fitness to exercise those they already possess, and will lead, as quickly as those proofs can be given, to a complete and final attainment of their status as the greatest Dominion in the British Commonwealth. It is to that end that we, British and Indians, have framed these proposals. We desire that the foundations of responsible government in India should be laid in trust and amity between her people and those whose forefathers have given this system to the world, that our enemies may learn that we know how to realize its principles, as well as to defend them. We, therefore, unite to submit this scheme, believing that so, in the Providence of God, a corner-stone may be laid in this Commonwealth of Nations for the perpetual union of East and West.

With regard to the details of the scheme outlined above, we think that it is desirable that every one should reserve full liberty of judgment. Our agreement relates only to the following specific points:—

We agree—

(1) to accept the pronouncement of the 20th of August as common ground, within the limits of which the discussion can take place;

(2) that, having accepted the pronouncement, we are not only free, but also bound to consider the new situation created thereby with open minds;

(3) that the existing provinces need not be assumed to be areas suitable as a basis for responsible government, but such areas must be settled at the moment when the first instalment of responsible government is granted;

(4) that the first steps towards responsible government cannot be taken in the sphere of the central Government;

(5) that, during the period of transition, governments of two types must co-exist, the one responsible to electorates for specific powers, the other to the Secretary of State for all other powers; that the responsibility of each must in fact be a real one, and their powers must be sufficient to enable them to discharge that responsibility efficiently;

(6) that a share of the consolidated revenue of the province should be handed over to the Provincial State Governments, proportionate to the cost of the functions transferred to them; in addition to which should be handed over certain specific powers of taxation, such as would fall on the Provincial State electorate itself;

(7) that further additions to the powers of Provincial States, and to their share of existing provincial revenues should be considered by Commissioners reporting direct to Parliament, at intervals of, say, seven years, such interval to be specified at the outset; and that in the intervening periods no demand for further executive powers, or for a further share of existing revenues, should be entertained;

(8) that legislation passed by Provincial State Governments affecting commercial and industrial undertakings should be reserved for the sanction of the Secretary of State; and a limit of time should be laid down, within which representations from the interests affected can be received by him; and further, that instructions to this effect should be included in a schedule attached to the Act of Parliament in which the scheme of reforms is embodied;

(9) that the Provincial Governments, responsible to the Government of India and the Secretary of State, shall have power to do or repair public works, upon which the value of invested capital depends, neglect of which is due to the default of Provincial State Governments, and to charge the cost thereof to the revenues assigned to the Government in default;

(10) that the Government of India must have the right to recall powers which have been abused or neglected; and in extreme cases to suspend the Governments of Provincial States. Such powers shall always be subject to the sanction of the Secretary of State and of Parliament; but in cases of emergency the Government of India may exercise the power, subject to subsequent sanction of the Secretary of State and of Parliament;

(11) that (*a*) wherever industrial and commercial interests are located, adequate representation should be accorded; (*b*) adequate representation should be accorded to Mahomedans, Land-holders, and minorities generally;

(12) that the specific points to which our agreement relates and the outlines of the scheme sketched in these proposals be laid down in an Act of Parliament: but that all questions within those outlines, relating to franchises, constitutions, powers, finances, and such like details be remitted to not more than five Commissioners named under the Act, to be dealt with in India by the Commissioners, in consultation with Governments and People, the arrangements of the Commissioners to be given the force of law by Orders in Council.

List of Signatories to the Joint Address received up to date Dec. 17, 1917.

1. C. B. Gregson.
2. G. Hennessy.
3. W. H. Arden Wood.
4. W. T. Grice.
5. A. R. Murray.
6. R. L. B. Gall.
7. James E. Roy.
8. A. D. Pickford.
9. J. Wyness.
10. W. R. Rae.
11. W. A Ironside
12. A. W. C. Chaplin.
13. A. J. Pugh.
14. W. H. Phelps.
15. Patt Lovett.
16. Thos. F. Tremearne.
17 Robert W. Brock.
18. C. R. Gebner.
19. T. R. Pratt.
20. Herbert Anderson.
21. H. B Eastwell.
22. Geo. E. Hicks.
23. A. P. Gray.
24. E. d'a Willis.
25. N. M. Ross.
26. Rev. A. E. Collier.
27. ,, P. N. F. Young
28. Wm. Hindle.
29. J. Mahdes.
30. R. W. Ellis.
31. Miss E. Goode.
32. Rev. B. Evans.
33. Rev. Josiah A. Ryburn
34. G. H. Kay.
35. Malcolm M. Crawford.
36. Rev. A. G. Hogg.
37. Roy D. Whitehorn.
38. J. H. Fowler.
39. H. D. B. Harford.
40 Rev. H. E. Clark.
41. James Lyon.
42. J. Broughton.
43. J. N. Jacobi.
44. W. E. S. Holland.
45. C. F. Beadel.
46. H. St. V. Chancellor.
47. Rev. Chas. D. Donald.
48. Gordon S. Wilkins.
49. C. D. Fraser.
50. Ian H. B. Stewart.
51. E. P. W. Nicholl.
52. Christopher Blomfield.
53. A. Yule.
54. F. Nelson Didsbury.
55. D. Sumerville.
56. F. R. Stevenson.
57. W. Stenhouse.
58. C. Westmacott.
59. A. B. Johnston.
60. Bernard Lucas.
61. T. V. Campbell.
62. H. Martyn Newton.
63. A. M. Newton.
64. J. D. Omond.

1. Bijoy Chand Mahtab, Maharajadhiraja Bahadur of Burdwan.
2. Maharaja Sir Prodyat Kumar Tagore.
3. Kshaunish Chandra Roy, Maharaja Bahadur of Nadia.

Girija Nath Roy, Maharaja Bahadur of Dinajpur.

5. Sir K. G. Gupta.
6. Nawab Serajul Islam.
7. Rajah Kisori Lal Goswami.
8 Provash Chunder Mitter.

Surendra Nath Roy.

10. Bhobendra Chunder Roy.

11. S. R. Dass.
12. B. C. Mitter.
13. S. C. Roy Chaudhuri.
14. Amulya Dhone Addy.
15. T. P. Ghose.
16. R. D. Mehta
17. Shib Shikareswar Roy.
18. S. Mahboob Ally.
19. A. Suhrawardy.
20. K. B. Dutt.
21. Bijoy Chatterjee.
22. H. D. Bose.
23. C. C. Ghose.
24. B. L. Mitter.
25. R. C. Bonnerjee.
26. R. S. Bajpai.
27. R. H M. Rustomjee.
28. D. Adhya.
29. Gobardhan Addya.
30. N. Gupta.
31. Jugal Kishore Ghose.
32. Nawab A. F. M. Abdur Rahman, Khan Bahadur.
33. S. M. Bose.
34. A Goswami.
35. H. Mullick.
36. H. C. Majumdar.
37. S. N. Banerjee.
38. Aroon Sinha.
39. R. N. Mitter.
40. P. N. Dutt.
41. N. N. Sircar
42 Ramendra Krishna Ghose.
43. Protap Chandra Mukerji, Rai Saheb.
44. Rajendra Chandra Chatterjee.
45. Surendra Chandra Chatterjee.
46. Srikanto Kumar Dey.
47. Tarini Charan Das.
48. Hara Lal Chattopadhyaya.
49. Saroda Kant Bandopadhyaya.
50. Mehruddin.
51. Arshed Ali.
52. Nemai Charan Dhopi.
53. Amar Charan Das.
54. The Hon'ble Rajah Kushalpal Sing.
55. N. Ghatak.
56. K. T. Paul.
57. Priya Nath Mallik.
58. Nivaran Chandra Dutta.
59. Jotish Chandra Mitter.
60. Rai Bahadur Manilal Nahar.
61. J. N Bose.
62. Giris Chandra Chakravarti.
63. Lal Mohan Sarkel.
64. Rai Hariram Goenka Bahadur, C.I.E.
65. Rajah Monmatha Nath Roy Chaudhury, of Santosh.
66. Rajah S. K. Acharya Bahadur, of Mymensingh.
67. Jitendra Kishore Acharya Chaudhury.
68. Aminuddin Hyder Faridie, M.R.A.G.S., F.R.H.S. (London).
69. D. C. Ghose.
70. H. M. Bose.
71. Siva Kali Kumar.
72. Hon. Abdur Rahim.
73. Sudhendu Mohan Bagchi.
74. Kishory Mohan Bagchi.
75. Lakshmipate Choudhure.
76. Ramprosad Bagchi.
77. Kishori Mohan Bagchi.
78. Surendra Mohan Maitra.
79. G. H. C. Ariff
80. Khan Bahadur Nawabjada Sayed Ashrafuddin Ahmed
81. Mahomedali Mamoojee.
82. Abu Musa Ahmadu'l Hoqq.
83. Joonas Oosman.
84. Yaccob C. Ariff.
85. Elias Muthrodan.
86. Moses Ambat.
87. Alphai Kallon.
88. Raja Gopal Lall Roy of Tajhat.
89. Indar Jogendra Singh.
90 T. Sriman Kantimatinathan.